The Gluten-Free Air Fryer Cookbook

100 Delicious and Easy Recipes for Your Air Fryer

COPYRIGHT

All rights reserved.

No part of this book may be reproduced in any form or by any electronic or mechanical means, including information storage and retrieval systems, without permission in writing from the publisher, except by a reviewer who may quote brief passages in a review.

The information contained in this book is based on the author's research and experience. While the author has made every effort to provide accurate and up-to-date information, errors and omissions may occur. The author and publisher assume no responsibility for any errors or omissions or for any actions taken based on the information contained in this book.

The information contained in this book is provided "as is," without warranty of any kind, express or implied, including but not limited to the warranties of merchantability, fitness for a particular purpose, or non-infringement. In no event shall the author or publisher be liable for any claim, damages, or other liability, whether in an action of contract, tort, or otherwise, arising from, out of, or in connection with the book or the use or other dealings in the book.

TABLE OF CONTENTS

INTRODUCTION 10

CHAPTER ONE 13

What is an air fryer? 13

What is the gluten free diet? 15

Benefits of the gluten free diet 17

Why air fryers are a useful kitchen appliance for gluten-free cooking? 20

Air fryer cooking techniQues and safety precautions .. 24

Air Fryer Cooking Techniques 24

Safety Precautions 25

The essential tools and ingredients needed for gluten-free air frying 27

Essential Tools 28

Essential Ingredients 29

Substitute for the above listed ingredients 31

Substitutes for Gluten-Free Flours 31

Substitutes for Gluten-Free Breadcrumbs 32

Substitutes for Gluten-Free Sweeteners 33

Substitutes for Dairy or Non-Dairy Ingredients 33

Substitutes for Gluten-Free Grains and Legumes................................ 34

Gluten intolerance or celiac disease. 35

Celiac Disease 35

Gluten Intolerance (Non-Celiac Gluten Sensitivity) 36

The importance of cross-contamination and how to avoid it in the kitchen. 38

Importance of Cross-Contamination 38

Ways to Avoid Cross-Contamination 39

How an air fryer works and its benefits. 41

How an Air Fryer Works 42

Benefits of Using an Air Fryer 42

Tips on preheating, temperature settings, and cooking times for various foods. 45

Alternative ingredients or substitutions to accommodate different dietary preferences 48

Vegan and Vegetarian 48

Gluten-Free 49

Paleo 49

Keto 50

Low-Sodium 51

Low-Carb 51

Tips for achieving the best results with an air fryer 52

Common issues that people might face when cooking with an air fryer or following a gluten-free diet............ 55

   Cooking with an Air Fryer 55

   Following a Gluten-Free Diet.. 56

Solutions to the above issues 58

   Cooking with an Air Fryer 58

   Following a Gluten-Free Diet.. 59

Advice on creating balanced and delicious gluten-free air-fried meals. 61

Advice on adjusting recipes or modifying cooking times. 64

Tips and tricks for successful gluten-free air frying. 68

CHAPTER TWO 71

   RECIPES.. 71

      Gluten-Free Air-Fried Chicken Tenders 71

      Crispy Air-Fried Gluten-Free Onion Rings 72

      Gluten-Free Air-Fried Sweet Potato Fries 73

      Air-Fried Gluten-Free Salmon with Herb Crust 73

      Gluten-Free Air-Fried Veggie Spring Rolls.......................... 74

      Gluten-Free Air-Fried Coconut Shrimp................................ 75

      Gluten-Free Air-Fried Avocado Fries 76

Air-Fried Gluten-Free Chicken and Vegetable Skewers................... 77
Gluten-Free Air-Fried Quinoa-Stuffed Peppers............................. 78
Gluten-Free Air-Fried Zucchini Chips 79
Gluten-Free Air-Fried Vegetable Fritters 80
Gluten-Free Air-Fried Stuffed Mushrooms 81
Gluten-Free Air-Fried Eggplant Parmesan 82
Gluten-Free Air-Fried Tofu with Peanut Sauce 83
Gluten-Free Air-Fried Banana Fritters....................................... 84
Gluten-Free Air-Fried Calamari Rings....................................... 85
Gluten-Free Air-Fried Shrimp Tacos 86
Gluten-Free Air-Fried Mac and Cheese Bites 86
Gluten-Free Air-Fried Stuffed Peppers 87
Gluten-Free Air-Fried Apple Cinnamon Donuts 88
Gluten-Free Air-Fried Buffalo Cauliflower Bites.......................... 89
Gluten-Free Air-Fried Beef and Vegetable Stir-Fry...................... 90
Gluten-Free Air-Fried Stuffed Mushrooms with Spinach and Cheese 91
Gluten-Free Air-Fried Fish Tacos 92
Gluten-Free Air-Fried Chocolate Brownie Bites 93
Gluten-Free Air-Fried Zesty Lemon Chicken 94
Gluten-Free Air-Fried Stuffed Bell Peppers with Quinoa and Black Beans.. 95
Gluten-Free Air-Fried Stuffed Apples with Cinnamon and Pecans. 96
Gluten-Free Air-Fried Garlic Herb Shrimp Skewers 96
Gluten-Free Air-Fried Stuffed Tomatoes with Quinoa and Feta...... 97

Gluten-Free Air-Fried Coconut Crusted Tilapia 98
Gluten-Free Air-Fried Sweet Chili Chicken Wings 99
Gluten-Free Air-Fried Asparagus with Parmesan 100
Gluten-Free Air-Fried Stuffed Bell Peppers with Rice and Ground Turkey 101
Gluten-Free Air-Fried Cheesy Garlic Breadsticks 102
Gluten-Free Air-Fried Stuffed Portobello Mushrooms 103
Gluten-Free Air-Fried Thai Basil Tofu 103
Gluten-Free Air-Fried Brussel Sprouts with Balsamic Glaze 104
Gluten-Free Air-Fried Chicken Parmesan 105
Gluten-Free Air-Fried Banana and Blueberry Muffins 106
Gluten-Free Air-Fried Mozzarella Sticks 107
Gluten-Free Air-Fried Stuffed Acorn Squash 108
Gluten-Free Air-Fried Ratatouille 109
Gluten-Free Air-Fried Chocolate-Covered Strawberries 110
Gluten-Free Air-Fried Stuffed Bell Peppers with Rice and Black Beans 111
Gluten-Free Air-Fried Sweet Potato Fries 112
Gluten-Free Air-Fried Stuffed Mushrooms with Spinach and Bacon 113
Gluten-Free Air-Fried Chicken Tenders with Honey Mustard Sauce 114
Gluten-Free Air-Fried Cinnamon Sugar Apple Chips 115
Gluten-Free Air-Fried Shrimp Po' Boy Sandwich 115
Gluten-Free Air-Fried Stuffed Avocado with Quinoa and Salsa 116

Gluten-Free Air-Fried Stuffed Eggplant with Italian Sausage and Cheese 117

Gluten-Free Air-Fried Potato Latkes 118

Gluten-Free Air-Fried Pineapple and Shrimp Skewers 119

Gluten-Free Air-Fried Green Bean Fries 120

Gluten-Free Air-Fried Stuffed Bell Peppers with Quinoa and Vegetables 121

Gluten-Free Air-Fried Garlic Herb Hasselback Potatoes 121

Gluten-Free Air-Fried BBQ Chicken Drumsticks 122

Gluten-Free Air-Fried Banana Walnut Bread 123

Gluten-Free Air-Fried Falafel 124

Gluten-Free Air-Fried Stuffed Zucchini Boats 125

Gluten-Free Air-Fried Teriyaki Tofu and Vegetable Skewers 126

Gluten-Free Air-Fried Stuffed Artichokes 127

Gluten-Free Air-Fried Cinnamon Sugar Donuts 127

Gluten-Free Air-Fried Stuffed Bell Peppers with Mexican Rice and Black Beans 128

Gluten-Free Air-Fried Stuffed Portobello Mushrooms with Spinach and Feta 129

Gluten-Free Air-Fried Buffalo Cauliflower Bites 130

Gluten-Free Air-Fried Pork Chops 131

Gluten-Free Air-Fried Brussels Sprouts with Bacon 132

Gluten-Free Air-Fried Stuffed Chicken Breasts with Spinach and Sun-Dried Tomatoes 133

Gluten-Free Air-Fried Cilantro-Lime Shrimp Tacos 134

Gluten-Free Air-Fried Chocolate Lava Cakes.................................. 135

Gluten-Free Air-Fried Buffalo Cauliflower Tacos........................... 135

Gluten-Free Air-Fried Zucchini Noodles with Pesto and Cherry Tomatoes.. 137

Gluten-Free Air-Fried Stuffed Sweet Potatoes with Chickpeas and Tahini Sauce.. 138

Gluten-Free Air-Fried Lemon Pepper Shrimp and Asparagus....... 138

Gluten-Free Air-Fried Coconut Chicken Tenders........................... 139

Gluten-Free Air-Fried Stuffed Mushrooms with Crab and Cream Cheese... 140

Gluten-Free Air-Fried Mozzarella Sticks... 141

Gluten-Free Air-Fried Garlic Parmesan Chicken Wings................ 142

Gluten-Free Air-Fried Avocado Fries 143

Gluten-Free Air-Fried Stuffed Acorn Squash with Quinoa and Cranberries... 144

Gluten-Free Air-Fried Greek Chicken Souvlaki Skewers................ 145

CONCLUSION 146

INTRODUCTION

Welcome to the "Complete Guide to Air Fryer Gluten-Free Recipes." In this comprehensive guide, we aim to take you on a culinary journey that combines the convenience and versatility of air frying with the health-conscious and delicious world of gluten-free cooking. Whether you are a seasoned home chef or just beginning to explore the joys of gluten-free cuisine, this guide is designed to empower you with the knowledge and skills to create delectable dishes that not only meet your dietary needs but also tantalize your taste buds.

For many individuals, adhering to a gluten-free diet is a necessity due to gluten intolerance or celiac disease. This dietary restriction can sometimes feel limiting, especially when it comes to enjoying crispy, fried foods. That's where the air fryer comes to the rescue. With its ability to mimic the texture and flavor of deep-frying while using minimal oil, the air fryer offers a perfect solution for those seeking gluten-free alternatives without compromising on taste and texture.

This guide is here to demystify the art of gluten-free air frying and help you master this cooking method. Whether you're looking to whip up crowd-pleasing appetizers, wholesome main courses, irresistible sides, or delightful desserts, we've got you covered. Our collection of tried-and-true recipes includes a wide range of dishes, each carefully crafted to be gluten-free, easy to follow, and guaranteed to satisfy even the most discerning palates.

Beyond the wonders of the air fryer, we delve into the world of gluten-free living. Whether by choice or necessity, adopting a gluten-free diet has gained traction for its potential benefits. For individuals with gluten intolerance or celiac disease, eliminating gluten is crucial for maintaining optimal health. But even for those without specific dietary restrictions, exploring gluten-free options can lead to improved digestion, increased energy levels, and a broader culinary palate.

We'll start with the basics, including essential tools, ingredients, and tips for successful air frying. We'll also delve into the nuances of gluten-free cooking, from understanding cross-contamination to making informed choices when it comes to gluten-free flours and breadcrumbs.

So, if you're ready to embark on a culinary adventure that's both delicious and dietary-friendly, let's dive into the world of gluten-free air frying. By the time you finish this guide, you'll not only have a repertoire of gluten-free air fryer recipes at your fingertips but also the confidence to get creative in your own kitchen. Get ready to savor the taste of gluten-free freedom with your air fryer!

CHAPTER ONE

WHAT IS AN AIR FRYER?

An air fryer is a kitchen appliance that cooks food by circulating hot air around it at high speed. It uses a convection mechanism to achieve a crispy exterior similar to frying, but with significantly less oil compared to traditional deep frying. The result is food that is both crispy and flavorful on the outside, while remaining moist and tender on the inside.

Here's how an air fryer typically works:

- Heating Element: The appliance has a powerful heating element that warms the air inside the cooking chamber.

- Fan: An integrated fan rapidly circulates the hot air, ensuring even cooking and crispiness.

- Cooking Basket: Food is placed in a perforated basket or tray that allows the hot air to circulate around it. This is where the cooking takes place.

- Temperature Control: Most air fryers come with adjustable temperature settings, allowing you to choose the desired cooking temperature for your specific recipe.

- Timer: You can set a timer to control how long your food cooks in the air fryer.

Air fryers are versatile appliances and can be used to cook a wide variety of foods, including but not limited to:

- French fries and other fried foods.

- Chicken wings and nuggets.

- Fish and seafood.

- Vegetables.

- Baked goods like cakes and muffins.

- Frozen convenience foods.

- Reheating leftovers.

The main advantage of using an air fryer is that it significantly reduces the amount of oil needed to achieve a crispy texture, making it a healthier alternative to deep frying. It's also faster than conventional ovens and produces less mess in the kitchen. Air fryers have gained popularity for their convenience and ability to cook foods with less added fat, making them a valuable addition to many kitchens.

WHAT IS THE GLUTEN FREE DIET?

A gluten-free diet is a dietary regimen that excludes the protein gluten. Gluten is found in grains such as wheat, barley, rye, and their derivatives. People choose or are prescribed a gluten-free diet for various reasons, the most common being:

- Celiac Disease: Celiac disease is an autoimmune disorder in which the ingestion of gluten triggers an immune response that damages the small intestine's lining. The only treatment for celiac disease is a strict, lifelong gluten-free diet.

- Non-Celiac Gluten Sensitivity: Some individuals experience symptoms similar to those of celiac disease when consuming gluten but do not test positive for celiac disease or a wheat allergy. They may have non-celiac gluten sensitivity, and they find relief from their symptoms by avoiding gluten.

- Wheat Allergy: A wheat allergy is an allergic reaction to proteins found in wheat, which can be different from celiac disease. People with a wheat allergy need to avoid wheat but may tolerate gluten-containing grains like barley and rye.

• Other Medical Conditions: In some cases, individuals with other medical conditions, such as certain autoimmune disorders or inflammatory bowel diseases, may be advised to follow a gluten-free diet to manage their condition.

A gluten-free diet involves eliminating all sources of gluten, which primarily means avoiding foods like:

• Wheat-based products, including bread, pasta, and cereal.

• Barley and barley-based products.

• Rye and rye-based products.

• Many processed foods that contain hidden sources of gluten, such as sauces, soups, and prepackaged meals.

To maintain a balanced and healthy diet while going gluten-free, individuals often substitute gluten-containing grains with alternatives like:

• Gluten-Free Grains: Such as rice, corn, quinoa, and oats (labeled gluten-free).

- Gluten-Free Flour: Including rice flour, almond flour, coconut flour, and gluten-free flour blends.

- Legumes and Pulses: Beans, lentils, and chickpeas are naturally gluten-free and can be used to prepare various dishes.

- Fresh Fruits and Vegetables: These are naturally gluten-free and are essential for a balanced diet.

It's important for individuals on a gluten-free diet to carefully read food labels, as gluten can hide in various processed and packaged foods. Gluten-free products are available in many grocery stores to help those on a gluten-free diet enjoy foods they might otherwise have to forgo.

If you suspect you have celiac disease, non-celiac gluten sensitivity, or a wheat allergy, it's important to consult with a healthcare professional for a proper diagnosis and guidance on managing your diet.

BENEFITS OF THE GLUTEN FREE DIET

The benefits of a gluten-free diet can vary depending on an individual's specific health needs and circumstances. While a gluten-free diet is essential for those with celiac disease or gluten-related disorders, it may offer other potential advantages for certain individuals. Here are some of the benefits associated with a gluten-free diet:

• Management of Celiac Disease: For individuals with celiac disease, the primary and most crucial benefit of a gluten-free diet is the management of their condition. It helps prevent the immune system response and intestinal damage triggered by gluten ingestion, leading to improved overall health.

• Relief from Gluten Sensitivity: People with non-celiac gluten sensitivity may experience digestive and non-digestive symptoms when they consume gluten. By eliminating gluten from their diet, they can find relief from these symptoms, such as abdominal discomfort, fatigue, and headaches.

• Reduction in Gastrointestinal Distress: Some individuals without diagnosed gluten-related disorders may find that a gluten-free diet alleviates gastrointestinal discomfort or bloating. This can be due to a reduction in hard-to-digest wheat products.

- Weight Management: A gluten-free diet may contribute to weight management for some individuals. By avoiding certain high-calorie, high-carb, and processed gluten-containing foods, they may consume fewer calories and make healthier food choices.

- Increased Awareness of Diet: Following a gluten-free diet often leads to increased awareness of food choices. Individuals are more likely to read food labels, select whole, unprocessed foods, and pay closer attention to their overall diet.

- Improved Digestive Health: Some people find that eliminating gluten helps with digestive issues, such as irritable bowel syndrome (IBS) or Crohn's disease, as gluten can be a trigger for gastrointestinal symptoms in certain individuals.

- Possible Enhanced Nutritional Quality: A gluten-free diet may encourage individuals to explore and incorporate nutrient-dense alternatives like fruits, vegetables, lean proteins, and naturally gluten-free grains, leading to a more balanced and nutritious diet.

- Potential Reduction in Inflammation: Some individuals with autoimmune or inflammatory conditions may experience a reduction in inflammation and associated symptoms on a gluten-free diet. However, this benefit can vary widely from person to person.

It's important to note that a gluten-free diet may have its drawbacks. It can be challenging to maintain, potentially more expensive, and may lead to nutritional deficiencies if not planned carefully. People considering a gluten-free diet for reasons other than medical necessity should consult with a healthcare provider or registered dietitian to ensure they maintain a balanced and nutritious diet.

If you suspect you have celiac disease, gluten sensitivity, or any other health condition related to gluten, it's essential to seek a professional diagnosis and guidance on managing your diet.

WHY AIR FRYERS ARE A USEFUL KITCHEN APPLIANCE FOR GLUTEN-FREE COOKING?

Air fryers are a useful kitchen appliance for gluten-free cooking for several reasons:

- Crispy Texture with Less Oil: Air fryers use a convection mechanism to circulate hot air rapidly around the food, providing a crispy exterior similar to deep-frying. This is achieved with only a fraction of the oil used in traditional frying methods. For gluten-free individuals, this means enjoying the satisfying crunch without the need for gluten-containing coatings.

- Healthier Cooking: Since air fryers require minimal oil to achieve that crispiness, they promote a healthier cooking method. This is especially beneficial for those with gluten-related disorders or other health concerns, as it reduces unnecessary fat and calories in their diet.

- Versatility: Air fryers can be used to cook a wide range of foods, making them a versatile appliance for gluten-free cooking. You can prepare everything from gluten-free chicken tenders to crispy vegetables, French fries, and even gluten-free baked goods, all in one appliance.

- Reduced Cross-Contamination: Cross-contamination is a significant concern for those with celiac disease or gluten sensitivity. When deep-frying in shared oil or using shared fryers, the risk of gluten cross-contamination is high. With an air fryer, you have control over what goes into the cooking basket, reducing the risk of contamination.

• Efficiency and Speed: Air fryers are efficient and cook food relatively quickly, making them a time-saving appliance in the kitchen. This is advantageous for individuals with busy lifestyles who need to prepare gluten-free meals efficiently.

• Consistent Results: Air fryers provide consistent and reliable results, ensuring that gluten-free foods come out evenly cooked and delicious. This consistency is especially important when dealing with gluten-free flours, which can behave differently from wheat flour.

• Customizable Recipes: Many air fryer recipes are naturally gluten-free or can be easily adapted. Air fryer cookbooks often include gluten-free options, allowing individuals to explore various gluten-free recipes with ease.

• Reduction in Frying Odors: Air fryers tend to produce fewer frying odors compared to traditional frying methods, which can be advantageous in households where individuals may be sensitive to cooking smells.

- Cost Savings: Preparing gluten-free fried foods at home with an air fryer can be more cost-effective than purchasing gluten-free equivalents from specialty stores or restaurants, which can be expensive.

- Wide Availability of Gluten-Free Ingredients: With the increasing demand for gluten-free products, there is now a wide range of gluten-free flours, breadcrumbs, and other ingredients readily available, making it easier to adapt recipes for the air fryer.

In summary, air fryers offer a convenient, healthy, and versatile way to prepare gluten-free meals. They enable individuals with dietary restrictions to enjoy the textures and flavors of fried foods without the risk of gluten cross-contamination or the need for excessive amounts of oil. This makes air fryers a valuable addition to the kitchen for those following a gluten-free diet.

AIR FRYER COOKING TECHNIQUES AND SAFETY PRECAUTIONS

Air fryer cooking can be a fantastic way to prepare a variety of dishes quickly and with less oil. To make the most of your air fryer while ensuring safety, here are some essential cooking techniques and safety precautions:

Air Fryer Cooking Techniques:

• Preheat the Air Fryer: Many air fryers require preheating for best results. Preheating helps food cook more evenly and develop a crispy exterior.

• Use the Right Temperature: Pay attention to the recommended cooking temperature for each recipe. Adjust the temperature according to the specific requirements of your dish.

• Don't Overcrowd the Basket: To achieve the crispiest results, avoid overcrowding the air fryer basket. Leave enough space for air to circulate around the food. Cook in batches if necessary.

• Use a Light Coating of Oil: While air fryers use less oil than traditional frying, a light coating of oil or cooking spray can enhance the texture and flavor of your dishes. Use an oil with a high smoke point, such as canola or grapeseed oil.

• Shake or Flip the Food: To ensure even cooking, shake or flip the food halfway through the cooking time. This helps prevent one side from becoming overly crispy while the other remains undercooked.

• Check for Doneness: Regularly check your food's progress during cooking. You can open the air fryer and check without disrupting the cooking process. Adjust the cooking time as needed.

• Use Accessories Wisely: Many air fryers come with accessories like racks or skewers. Use these as needed for specific recipes, but be cautious not to block the airflow.

Safety Precautions:

• Read the Manual: Familiarize yourself with your specific air fryer's user manual. Different models have varying settings and features.

- Place on a Heat-Resistant Surface: Ensure that your air fryer is positioned on a heat-resistant, flat, and stable surface to prevent accidental tipping.

- Keep It Clean: Regularly clean the air fryer's removable parts, including the basket and pan. This prevents the buildup of residue that can cause smoking or unpleasant odors.

- Prevent Oil Splatter: When removing the basket or tray, be cautious to avoid any hot oil splatter. Wear oven mitts or use tongs if necessary.

- Don't Block Ventilation: Ensure that the air fryer's vents and openings are not obstructed during operation. Proper ventilation prevents overheating.

- Avoid Water in the Basket: Never place wet or damp items in the air fryer, as it can lead to splattering, smoking, and damage to the appliance.

- Watch for Smoke: If you notice excessive smoke during cooking, immediately turn off the air fryer and unplug it. Smoke could indicate an issue, such as oil dripping onto the heating element.

- Allow Cooling Time: After use, allow the air fryer to cool down before cleaning or storing it. The interior can remain hot even after cooking.

- Use Heat-Resistant Kitchen Tools: Use heat-resistant utensils, such as tongs or silicone spatulas, when handling food inside the air fryer.

- Unplug After Use: Always unplug the air fryer when it's not in use, especially if you have young children in the household.

By following these cooking techniques and safety precautions, you can enjoy the benefits of your air fryer while minimizing the risk of accidents and ensuring that your dishes turn out perfectly cooked.

THE ESSENTIAL TOOLS AND INGREDIENTS NEEDED FOR GLUTEN-FREE AIR FRYING.

To successfully air fry gluten-free dishes, you'll need a combination of essential tools and ingredients. Here's a list of what you should have in your kitchen:

Essential Tools:

• Air Fryer: The central piece of equipment, the air fryer, cooks food with hot, circulating air. Make sure to have a model that fits your needs and the types of dishes you plan to prepare.

• Measuring Cups and Spoons: Accurate measurement of ingredients is essential in gluten-free cooking to ensure the right texture and taste in your dishes.

• Oil Sprayer or Brush: For applying a light coating of oil to food items, helping them crisp up during air frying. Look for oil sprayers designed to work with high-heat cooking.

• Parchment Paper or Perforated Parchment Liners: To prevent sticking and simplify cleanup, you can use parchment paper or specifically designed perforated parchment liners for the air fryer basket.

• Silicone Tongs or Kitchen Utensils: Non-metallic kitchen tools are ideal for air fryer use to avoid damaging the non-stick coating in the basket.

- Digital Kitchen Thermometer: It's useful for checking the internal temperature of meats and baked goods, ensuring they are cooked to perfection.

- Cooking Spray: A gluten-free cooking spray, such as a canola or olive oil spray, can be used to lightly coat the air fryer basket or food to prevent sticking.

Essential Ingredients:

- Gluten-Free Flours: These are the foundation of many gluten-free recipes. Common options include rice flour, almond flour, coconut flour, and gluten-free all-purpose flour blends. Select the one that suits your recipe best.

- Gluten-Free Breadcrumbs: Use gluten-free breadcrumbs, which are often made from rice flour, cornstarch, or other gluten-free grains, as an alternative to traditional breadcrumbs for coating.

- Proteins: You can prepare a wide variety of proteins in the air fryer, such as chicken, fish, shrimp, and tofu. Ensure they are fresh and gluten-free, and consider marinating them for added flavor.

• Vegetables: Many vegetables, such as potatoes, zucchini, and Brussels sprouts, can be air-fried. Ensure they are clean and free from cross-contamination.

• Gluten-Free Seasonings: Common seasonings like salt, pepper, and herbs are naturally gluten-free. Check spice blends and seasonings for any hidden sources of gluten.

• Gluten-Free Sauces and Condiments: Be cautious with sauces and condiments, as some may contain gluten. Look for gluten-free alternatives to enhance the flavor of your dishes.

• Gluten-Free Starches: Ingredients like cornstarch and tapioca starch can be used as thickeners for sauces and gravies.

• Dairy or Non-Dairy Ingredients: If your recipe calls for dairy products, make sure they are gluten-free. For non-dairy alternatives, ensure they are labeled as gluten-free.

• Gluten-Free Sweeteners: For baking or sweet dishes, use gluten-free sweeteners like granulated sugar, brown sugar, or honey.

• Gluten-Free Grains and Legumes: When making side dishes, consider gluten-free grains like rice, quinoa, or gluten-free pasta. Legumes like lentils and chickpeas are also gluten-free and versatile.

Remember to read product labels carefully to verify that the ingredients are gluten-free, especially when using packaged items. Additionally, choose dedicated gluten-free products whenever possible to minimize the risk of cross-contamination. With the right tools and ingredients, you'll be well-prepared to create delicious gluten-free air-fried dishes.

SUBSTITUTE FOR THE ABOVE LISTED INGREDIENTS

Substituting ingredients in gluten-free cooking can be necessary due to dietary restrictions or allergies. Here are some common substitutes for the ingredients listed in gluten-free air frying:

Substitutes for Gluten-Free Flours:

- All-Purpose Gluten-Free Flour Blends: These commercially available blends are designed to replace wheat flour in most recipes. They typically contain a mix of gluten-free flours, starches, and xanthan gum for binding. Use them as a 1:1 substitute for wheat flour.

- Almond Flour: Almond flour is an excellent substitute for wheat flour in many recipes, especially those that require a nutty flavor and a moist texture. Keep in mind that almond flour behaves differently, so it may require additional binding agents like eggs.

- Coconut Flour: Coconut flour is another gluten-free option, but it's highly absorbent and may require more liquid in recipes. It imparts a subtle coconut flavor.

- Rice Flour: White or brown rice flour is a versatile gluten-free flour used in a variety of recipes, from baked goods to coatings for frying.

Substitutes for Gluten-Free Breadcrumbs:

- Gluten-Free Panko Breadcrumbs: Gluten-free panko breadcrumbs are available in most stores and work as a direct substitute for regular panko breadcrumbs.

- Crushed Cornflakes or Rice Cereal: For a crunchy coating, you can crush gluten-free cornflakes or rice cereal as a substitute for breadcrumbs.

- Ground Nuts or Seeds: Ground nuts (like almonds) or seeds (like sunflower or pumpkin seeds) can be used to create a gluten-free coating with added texture and flavor.

Substitutes for Gluten-Free Sweeteners:

- Granulated Sugar: Granulated sugar can be substituted with other granulated sweeteners like maple sugar, coconut sugar, or stevia for a lower-sugar option.

- Brown Sugar: Brown sugar can be replaced with coconut sugar, palm sugar, or a blend of molasses and granulated sugar for a similar depth of flavor.

Substitutes for Dairy or Non-Dairy Ingredients:

- Dairy-Free Milk: Non-dairy milk alternatives like almond, soy, rice, or coconut milk can replace cow's milk in recipes. Choose unsweetened and unflavored varieties.

- Vegan Butter or Margarine: If a recipe calls for butter or margarine, you can use dairy-free butter or margarine as a substitute.

- Non-Dairy Yogurt: Replace dairy yogurt with non-dairy alternatives like coconut, almond, or soy yogurt for recipes that require a dairy component.

Substitutes for Gluten-Free Grains and Legumes:

- Gluten-Free Pasta: There are various gluten-free pasta options available made from rice, corn, quinoa, chickpeas, or other grains. Choose the one that suits your dish.

- Gluten-Free Grains: Use gluten-free grains like quinoa, rice, or certified gluten-free oats as alternatives to wheat-based grains.

- Gluten-Free Starches: Tapioca starch, potato starch, or arrowroot powder can be used as thickeners in place of wheat-based starches like cornstarch.

- Legumes: Beans, lentils, and chickpeas are naturally gluten-free and can be used in various dishes.

Keep in mind that the success of these substitutes may vary depending on the specific recipe and intended dish. Always read labels carefully to ensure that the substitutes you choose are certified gluten-free and safe for your dietary needs.

Additionally, consider experimenting with different options to find the ones that work best for your desired flavor and texture in gluten-free air frying.

GLUTEN INTOLERANCE OR CELIAC DISEASE.

Gluten intolerance and celiac disease are related conditions that involve an adverse reaction to gluten, a protein found in wheat, barley, and rye. However, they are distinct conditions with different characteristics and implications.

Celiac Disease:

• Autoimmune Disorder: Celiac disease is an autoimmune disorder. When someone with celiac disease consumes gluten, their immune system reacts by damaging the lining of the small intestine. This immune response can lead to various health issues.

• Genetic Predisposition: Celiac disease has a strong genetic component, and it is more common in individuals with a family history of the condition. Not everyone with a genetic predisposition will develop celiac disease, but it increases the risk.

- Wide Range of Symptoms: Celiac disease can manifest with a wide range of symptoms, including digestive problems (e.g., diarrhea, abdominal pain), as well as non-digestive symptoms like fatigue, skin rashes, joint pain, and neurological symptoms.

- Diagnosis: Celiac disease can be diagnosed through blood tests measuring specific antibodies and confirmed with a biopsy of the small intestine. The gold standard for diagnosis is an endoscopic procedure known as an upper endoscopy.

- Treatment: The only effective treatment for celiac disease is a strict, lifelong gluten-free diet. Avoiding gluten helps prevent the immune system response and the damage to the small intestine.

Gluten Intolerance (Non-Celiac Gluten Sensitivity):

- Non-Autoimmune Condition: Gluten intolerance, also known as non-celiac gluten sensitivity (NCGS), is not an autoimmune condition. Instead, it's characterized by adverse reactions to gluten without the autoimmune response seen in celiac disease.

- Symptoms: People with gluten intolerance experience symptoms after consuming gluten, similar to those seen in celiac disease, such as gastrointestinal discomfort, fatigue, headaches, and joint pain. However, they do not test positive for celiac disease or wheat allergy.

• Lack of Biomarkers: Unlike celiac disease, gluten intolerance lacks clear biomarkers. There are no blood tests or specific diagnostic procedures to confirm the condition, making diagnosis based on symptom resolution after eliminating gluten and excluding other causes.

• Management: The primary management of gluten intolerance is the avoidance of gluten-containing foods. When gluten is removed from the diet, many individuals with NCGS find relief from their symptoms.

In summary, celiac disease is an autoimmune condition with a clear diagnostic process and specific biomarkers, while gluten intolerance (NCGS) is characterized by adverse reactions to gluten without the autoimmune component. Both conditions require individuals to adopt a gluten-free diet, but the reasons and implications for each differ. If you suspect you have either condition, it is essential to consult with a healthcare professional for proper evaluation and guidance.

THE IMPORTANCE OF CROSS-CONTAMINATION AND HOW TO AVOID IT IN THE KITCHEN.

Cross-contamination is a critical concern, especially for individuals with food allergies or dietary restrictions like celiac disease. It occurs when harmful microorganisms, allergens, or unwanted substances are transferred from one food item, surface, or utensil to another. In the context of dietary restrictions like gluten intolerance or celiac disease, cross-contamination with gluten-containing foods can have serious health consequences. Here's why it's important and how to avoid it in the kitchen:

Importance of Cross-Contamination:

- Health Risks: For individuals with celiac disease or gluten sensitivity, even tiny amounts of gluten can trigger adverse reactions, such as digestive issues, skin rashes, fatigue, and more. Long-term exposure to gluten can cause damage to the small intestine, leading to severe health complications.

- Allergen Concerns: Cross-contamination is also a significant issue for individuals with food allergies. Even trace amounts of allergens can lead to allergic reactions, which can range from mild discomfort to life-threatening situations.

• Quality of Life: Avoiding cross-contamination is essential for maintaining a good quality of life for those with dietary restrictions. It allows them to enjoy meals without constantly worrying about inadvertent exposure to allergens or gluten.

Ways to Avoid Cross-Contamination:

• Dedicated Kitchen Tools: Use separate kitchen utensils, cutting boards, and cookware for gluten-free and allergen-free cooking. Designate specific items for this purpose to reduce the risk of cross-contamination.

• Clean and Sanitize: Regularly clean and sanitize your kitchen surfaces, especially if they come into contact with gluten-containing foods. Pay close attention to shared appliances like toasters and food processors.

• Handwashing: Wash your hands thoroughly with soap and water before handling gluten-free or allergen-free foods. This is a simple yet effective way to prevent contamination.

- Labeling: Clearly label containers, both in the pantry and the refrigerator, to differentiate between gluten-free and non-gluten-free ingredients.

- Separate Storage: Store gluten-free and allergen-free foods separately from gluten-containing foods. Use sealed containers or bags to prevent cross-contamination.

- Prevent Airborne Contamination: Be cautious when using flour, as it can become airborne and settle on surfaces or other foods. Consider preparing gluten-free items first if you need to use wheat flour in the same cooking session.

- Avoid Bulk Bins: When shopping, avoid bulk bins that may carry the risk of cross-contamination. Opt for pre-packaged, certified gluten-free, or allergen-free products.

- Be Informed: Familiarize yourself with food labels and ingredient lists to identify hidden sources of gluten or allergens. Learn to recognize less obvious names for these ingredients.

- Communication: If dining out or attending social events, communicate your dietary needs to chefs, hosts, or waitstaff to ensure they are aware of your requirements.

- Educate Family and Friends: If you have dietary restrictions, educate your family and friends about the importance of cross-contamination and how to prepare safe meals when you visit their homes.

- Be Vigilant: Continue to be vigilant and proactive in your efforts to avoid cross-contamination. It's better to be safe than sorry.

Preventing cross-contamination is a continuous effort, but it's crucial for the health and well-being of individuals with dietary restrictions. By following these practices, you can significantly reduce the risk of unintended exposure to allergens or gluten.

HOW AN AIR FRYER WORKS AND ITS BENEFITS.

An air fryer is a kitchen appliance that works by circulating hot air around the food to cook it. It uses a convection mechanism to produce a crispy exterior, similar to frying, with significantly less oil than traditional deep frying. Here's how an air fryer works and its benefits:

How an Air Fryer Works:

• Heating Element: The air fryer has a heating element that warms the air inside the cooking chamber.

• Fan: An integrated fan rapidly circulates the hot air around the food. This forced convection creates an even cooking environment and ensures that the food is cooked on all sides.

• Cooking Basket or Tray: Food is placed in a perforated basket or on a tray, allowing the hot air to circulate around and through it. The basket or tray is usually removable for easy loading and cleaning.

• Temperature Control: Most air fryers come with adjustable temperature settings, allowing you to set the desired cooking temperature for your specific recipe.

• Timer: You can set a timer to control how long your food cooks in the air fryer. When the timer reaches zero, the appliance typically shuts off automatically.

Benefits of Using an Air Fryer:

• Healthier Cooking: The primary benefit of an air fryer is that it allows for healthier cooking. You can achieve the texture and taste of fried foods with significantly less oil, reducing the overall fat and calorie content of your dishes. This makes it a healthier alternative to deep frying.

• Crispy Texture: Air fryers excel at creating a crispy exterior on food, similar to the results of deep-frying. This crispy texture is achieved through the hot air circulation.

• Versatility: Air fryers are versatile appliances. They can cook a wide range of foods, from traditional fried items like chicken wings and French fries to roasting vegetables, baking goods, and reheating leftovers.

• Time Efficiency: Air fryers are faster than traditional ovens, making them a time-efficient option for cooking. They preheat quickly and often require shorter cooking times for various dishes.

• Reduced Odor: Air fryers produce fewer cooking odors than traditional frying methods, making them more suitable for indoor cooking without the lingering smell of fried foods.

• Ease of Use: Air fryers are user-friendly appliances with straightforward controls, making them accessible to both experienced and novice cooks.

- Easy Cleanup: Many air fryers have removable, dishwasher-safe parts, which simplifies cleanup. Additionally, the reduced use of oil minimizes grease splatter and residue in the kitchen.

- Economical: Preparing fried foods at home with an air fryer can be more cost-effective than dining out or purchasing pre-packaged fried products.

- Environmental Impact: Using an air fryer can be more environmentally friendly than traditional deep frying, as it generally consumes less energy and produces fewer emissions.

In summary, an air fryer is a valuable kitchen appliance that offers healthier cooking options, produces delicious crispy results, and provides versatility for a wide range of dishes. Its ability to mimic the texture and flavor of deep-frying while using minimal oil makes it a popular choice for those seeking a healthier and more convenient way to enjoy fried foods.

TIPS ON PREHEATING, TEMPERATURE SETTINGS, AND COOKING TIMES FOR VARIOUS FOODS.

Air fryers are versatile appliances that can cook a variety of foods, but achieving the best results often depends on preheating, temperature settings, and cooking times. Here are some tips for different foods:

1. Preheating:

Preheating the air fryer is not always necessary, but it can help in some cases. If you're cooking food that benefits from a crispy texture, like fries or chicken, consider preheating the air fryer for 2-3 minutes before adding the food.

2. Temperature Settings:

Different foods require different temperature settings. Here are some general guidelines:

• Chicken and Meat: Cook at 350-400°F (175-200°C) for about 12-25 minutes, depending on the cut and thickness. Use higher temperatures for a crispy crust and lower temperatures for even cooking.

- Frozen Foods: Many frozen items like French fries, chicken nuggets, and fish sticks can be cooked at 375-400°F (190-200°C) for 10-20 minutes.

- Vegetables: Roast vegetables at 375-400°F (190-200°C) for 10-20 minutes, depending on the type and size. Toss them in a little oil for extra crispiness.

- Baked Goods: For items like muffins or biscuits, bake at 325-350°F (160-175°C) for 10-20 minutes, depending on the recipe.

3. Cooking Times:

Cooking times can vary based on factors like the air fryer's wattage, the food's thickness, and personal preferences. It's essential to monitor the food and adjust the cooking time accordingly. Shake or flip the food halfway through the cooking time to ensure even results.

4. Additional Tips:

- Use a cooking spray: For foods that require a crispy exterior, lightly spray or brush them with oil to enhance the texture.

- Arrange in a single layer: Avoid overcrowding the air fryer basket, as this can hinder proper air circulation and result in uneven cooking.

- Use a meat thermometer: For meats, especially poultry and larger cuts, use a meat thermometer to ensure they reach a safe internal temperature.

- Check doneness: Check the food's doneness as it nears the end of the cooking time. Cooking times may vary based on the air fryer model and wattage.

- For battered or breaded foods: To prevent breading from sticking to the basket, place a piece of parchment paper or a perforated liner at the bottom. This also makes cleanup easier.

- For reheating: When reheating leftovers, use a lower temperature (around 250-300°F or 120-150°C) to prevent overcooking and maintain moisture.

Remember that air fryers can vary in their performance, so it's a good idea to become familiar with your specific model and adjust settings accordingly. Experimentation and practice will help you become more skilled at air frying different foods to perfection.

ALTERNATIVE INGREDIENTS OR SUBSTITUTIONS TO ACCOMMODATE DIFFERENT DIETARY PREFERENCES.

Accommodating different dietary preferences often requires alternative ingredients or substitutions to ensure that everyone can enjoy the same meal. Here are some common dietary preferences and suitable ingredient substitutions:

1. Vegan and Vegetarian:

• Meat: Substitute with plant-based protein sources like tofu, tempeh, seitan, or legumes (beans, lentils, chickpeas).

• Dairy: Replace dairy milk with almond, soy, oat, or coconut milk, and use non-dairy cheeses or nutritional yeast as a cheese alternative.

• Eggs: For binding in recipes, use flax or chia eggs (1 tablespoon ground flaxseed or chia seeds mixed with 3 tablespoons of water).

• Butter: Substitute with vegan butter or margarine, coconut oil, or applesauce for baking.

- Cream: Use coconut cream or cashew cream as a dairy-free alternative in savory or sweet dishes.

2. Gluten-Free:

- Flour: Replace wheat flour with gluten-free flours like rice flour, almond flour, coconut flour, or a gluten-free all-purpose flour blend.

- Breadcrumbs: Use certified gluten-free breadcrumbs or crushed gluten-free cereal.

- Soy Sauce: Substitute with gluten-free tamari or coconut aminos.

- Pasta: Choose gluten-free pasta made from rice, corn, quinoa, or other gluten-free grains.

- Baking Powder: Ensure that baking powder is labeled gluten-free, or use a mix of baking soda and cream of tartar.

3. Paleo:

Grains: Avoid grains and instead use almond flour, coconut flour, or tapioca flour for baking.

- Legumes: Exclude legumes and choose alternative protein sources like animal proteins, nuts, and seeds.

- Dairy: Limit or eliminate dairy and use ghee or coconut milk as dairy alternatives.

- Refined Sugar: Substitute refined sugars with natural sweeteners like honey, maple syrup, or coconut sugar.

- Processed Foods: Avoid processed foods and focus on whole, unprocessed ingredients.

4. Keto:

- Carbohydrates: Reduce or eliminate high-carb ingredients like wheat flour, sugar, and starchy vegetables.

- Healthy Fats: Incorporate healthy fats like avocado, olive oil, and coconut oil.

- Sugar: Use sugar substitutes like stevia, erythritol, or monk fruit sweetener.

- Flour: Choose almond flour, coconut flour, or flaxseed meal for baking and coating.

- Protein: Prioritize high-protein sources like meat, fish, eggs, and dairy (if not lactose-intolerant).

5. Low-Sodium:

- Salt: Reduce or eliminate salt and use alternative seasonings like herbs, spices, citrus, and low-sodium broth.

- Soy Sauce: Opt for reduced-sodium soy sauce or tamari.

- Canned Goods: Look for low-sodium or no-salt-added canned goods.

6. Low-Carb:

- Carbohydrates: Minimize carb-rich ingredients like rice, pasta, and bread. Use spiralized vegetables (zucchini noodles, spaghetti squash) or cauliflower rice as alternatives.

- Sugar: Use sugar substitutes like stevia, erythritol, or xylitol.

- Flour: Substitute with almond flour, coconut flour, or flaxseed meal for low-carb baking.

By incorporating these ingredient substitutions, you can cater to various dietary preferences and make your recipes more inclusive, allowing everyone to enjoy the same meal while adhering to their dietary needs.

TIPS FOR ACHIEVING THE BEST RESULTS WITH AN AIR FRYER

To achieve the best results with an air fryer, consider the following tips and techniques:

• Preheat Your Air Fryer (When Necessary): Some recipes benefit from preheating for a few minutes, especially if you want a crispy texture. Preheating ensures the air fryer is hot when you place the food inside.

• Arrange Food in a Single Layer: Avoid overcrowding the air fryer basket. Ensure there's enough space between food items to allow proper air circulation. Cook in batches if needed.

• Use a Light Coating of Oil: For foods that require a crispy exterior, lightly spray or brush them with oil. This helps achieve a better texture. Consider using an oil sprayer for even distribution.

- Shake or Flip Food: To ensure even cooking, shake the basket or flip the food halfway through the cooking time. This prevents one side from becoming overly crispy while the other remains undercooked.

- Monitor Doneness: As you near the end of the cooking time, check the food's progress. Cooking times can vary depending on the air fryer model, the thickness of the food, and personal preferences.

- Use Accessories Wisely: If your air fryer comes with accessories like racks, skewers, or baking pans, use them according to your specific recipe. Ensure they don't block airflow.

- Adjust Temperature and Time: Don't be afraid to experiment with temperature settings and cooking times to find the perfect balance for your specific dishes.

- Pre-Treat Certain Foods: Some foods, like potato wedges, benefit from being soaked in cold water for 30 minutes before air frying. This removes excess starch and improves crispiness.

- Avoid Wet or Damp Food: Don't place wet or damp food items in the air fryer, as it can lead to splattering, steaming, or an uneven texture. Pat dry food items before cooking.

- Don't Overload the Basket: Avoid overloading the basket with a large quantity of food, as it can hinder air circulation and result in uneven cooking. Ensure there's space for the hot air to move around the food.

- Read the Manual: Familiarize yourself with your specific air fryer's user manual. Different models have varying settings and features, so understanding how to use them is essential.

- Experiment: Every air fryer is different, and the best results often come from experimenting with different foods and settings. Don't be discouraged by initial attempts; practice will lead to better outcomes.

- Keep It Clean: Regularly clean the air fryer's removable parts, including the basket and pan. This prevents the buildup of residue, which can affect cooking and produce unpleasant odors.

By following these tips and adapting them to your specific air fryer model and recipes, you can achieve the best results and create delicious, crispy, and healthy dishes with your air fryer.

COMMON ISSUES THAT PEOPLE MIGHT FACE WHEN COOKING WITH AN AIR FRYER OR FOLLOWING A GLUTEN-FREE DIET

Cooking with an air fryer and following a gluten-free diet can have their challenges. Here are some common issues that people might face:

Cooking with an Air Fryer:

- Overcrowding: One of the most common issues is overcrowding the air fryer basket. Overcrowding can lead to uneven cooking and prevent the food from crisping up properly. It's essential to cook in batches if needed and leave space for air circulation.

- Food Sticking: Despite the non-stick coatings, some foods may still stick to the basket or tray. To prevent this, use parchment paper or a perforated liner for items like battered or breaded foods.

- Uneven Results: Achieving even results can be a challenge, as hot spots can develop in some air fryer models. To address this, rotate or shake the basket or tray during cooking for more consistent results.

- Drying Out: Certain foods, especially lean proteins like chicken breast, can become dry in the air fryer. To prevent this, marinate or brine the food beforehand, or use a meat thermometer to avoid overcooking.

- Adjusting to Different Models: Different air fryer models have varying wattages, sizes, and settings. Adjusting to a new model may require some experimentation to achieve the desired results.

- Noise Level: Some air fryers can be relatively noisy due to the fan and heating elements. This may be an issue for those who prefer quieter cooking appliances.

Following a Gluten-Free Diet:

- Cross-Contamination: Avoiding cross-contamination with gluten-containing foods can be challenging, particularly in shared kitchens. Ensuring a dedicated cooking area and separate utensils is crucial.

- Hidden Gluten: Gluten can hide in unexpected places, such as sauces, seasonings, and processed foods. Reading labels and asking questions when dining out is essential to avoid hidden sources of gluten.

- Limited Dining Options: Dining out or ordering takeout can be more challenging for individuals on a gluten-free diet. Many restaurants are now offering gluten-free menus, but cross-contamination remains a concern.

- Social Situations: Social events and gatherings often involve shared food. It can be challenging to navigate these situations, as others may not fully understand gluten-free dietary needs.

- Expense: Some gluten-free products can be more expensive than their gluten-containing counterparts, which may be a financial concern for those on a gluten-free diet.

- Taste and Texture: Achieving the same taste and texture in gluten-free recipes can be challenging. Baking, in particular, can require experimentation with different flours and binders to achieve the desired results.

To address these issues, it's important to be well-informed and prepared. For those using air fryers, understanding the specific model and experimenting with different recipes can lead to better results. For individuals following a gluten-free diet, staying diligent about cross-contamination, reading labels, and educating others about their dietary needs are essential steps to ensure a safe and enjoyable dining experience.

SOLUTIONS TO THE ABOVE ISSUES

Here are some solutions to the common issues people might face when cooking with an air fryer and following a gluten-free diet:

Cooking with an Air Fryer:

• Overcrowding: Cook in batches and leave space for air circulation. This may take a little more time, but it ensures even results.

• Food Sticking: Use parchment paper or perforated liners for foods that tend to stick. Some models also have non-stick cooking sprays designed for air frying.

- Uneven Results: Rotate or shake the basket or tray during cooking to promote even cooking. Familiarize yourself with your specific air fryer's hot spots.

- Drying Out: To prevent dryness, marinate proteins before cooking, use a meat thermometer, and avoid overcooking. You can also add a little liquid or sauce to help keep the food moist.

- Adjusting to Different Models: Refer to the user manual for your specific air fryer model to understand its settings and features. Experiment with cooking times and temperatures to achieve your desired results.

- Noise Level: Consider the noise level when choosing an air fryer. Some models are quieter than others, so select one that suits your preference for noise.

Following a Gluten-Free Diet:

- Cross-Contamination: Maintain a dedicated gluten-free cooking area with separate utensils and cutting boards. Designate specific storage areas for gluten-free ingredients to avoid accidental cross-contact.

- Hidden Gluten: Read food labels diligently to identify hidden sources of gluten. Learn to recognize gluten-containing ingredients and always inquire about preparation methods when dining out.

- Limited Dining Options: Research restaurants that offer gluten-free menus or cater to dietary restrictions. Communicate your needs to restaurant staff, and be prepared to ask questions about ingredients and cooking procedures.

- Social Situations: Educate friends and family about your dietary needs, and consider bringing your own gluten-free dish to social gatherings to ensure you have safe options to enjoy.

- Expense: To manage the cost, focus on naturally gluten-free foods like fruits, vegetables, lean proteins, and whole grains like rice and quinoa. Purchase gluten-free products in bulk or when they are on sale.

- Taste and Texture: Experiment with gluten-free flours and starches to achieve the desired taste and texture in your recipes. Blend different flours or use binders like xanthan gum or psyllium husk to mimic gluten's properties.

By implementing these solutions, you can overcome the common challenges associated with cooking in an air fryer and following a gluten-free diet, ensuring you have delicious and safe culinary experiences.

ADVICE ON CREATING BALANCED AND DELICIOUS GLUTEN-FREE AIR-FRIED MEALS.

Creating balanced and delicious gluten-free air-fried meals requires attention to both nutrition and flavor. Here's some advice on how to achieve this:

• Start with Fresh, Whole Ingredients: Choose whole foods like lean proteins, fresh vegetables, and whole grains as the foundation of your meals.

• Include a Protein Source: Incorporate lean proteins such as chicken, turkey, fish, tofu, or legumes for a satisfying meal. Marinate or season the protein to add flavor.

• Add Veggies: Vegetables are rich in nutrients and add color and flavor to your meal. Season and lightly oil them before air frying for extra taste.

- Use Gluten-Free Grains: If you want to include grains, opt for gluten-free options like quinoa, rice, or gluten-free pasta. Cook them separately and add them to your air-fried dish.

- Flavor with Herbs and Spices: Fresh herbs, spices, and gluten-free seasonings can elevate the taste of your meals without the need for gluten-containing sauces. Experiment with various flavor profiles.

- Healthy Fats: Include sources of healthy fats like avocado, olive oil, nuts, or seeds to enhance flavor and provide satiety.

- Avoid Gluten-Containing Sauces: Be cautious with sauces and condiments, as many contain gluten. Opt for gluten-free alternatives or make your own sauces from scratch.

- Pay Attention to Portions: Be mindful of portion sizes to ensure balanced meals. Overloading your air fryer can lead to uneven cooking.

- Experiment with Gluten-Free Breading: Try gluten-free breadcrumbs, crushed gluten-free cereal, or almond flour for coating. Use your air fryer to achieve a crispy texture.

• Monitor Cooking Times: Keep a close eye on cooking times to prevent overcooking. Use a meat thermometer for proteins to ensure they reach safe internal temperatures.

• Combine Textures: Create a balance of textures in your meal. For example, pair a crispy protein with tender vegetables or a creamy sauce.

• Add Freshness: Incorporate fresh elements like a side salad with a gluten-free vinaigrette to provide a contrasting, refreshing element.

• Don't Forget Dessert: You can also air fry gluten-free desserts. Explore recipes for air-fried apple slices, gluten-free donuts, or other sweet treats.

• Hydration: Accompany your meal with water or a gluten-free beverage of your choice to stay hydrated.

• Plan Balanced Meals: When meal planning, ensure a balance of protein, carbohydrates, and healthy fats to meet your dietary needs and preferences.

- Be Creative: Don't be afraid to experiment and get creative with your gluten-free air-fried meals. Try new ingredients, flavors, and combinations.

Creating balanced and delicious gluten-free air-fried meals is a matter of choosing fresh, wholesome ingredients, using herbs and spices for flavor, and paying attention to cooking techniques. With practice and experimentation, you can develop a repertoire of gluten-free air-fried recipes that are both nutritious and satisfying.

ADVICE ON ADJUSTING RECIPES OR MODIFYING COOKING TIMES.

Adapting recipes or modifying cooking times is often necessary when using an air fryer, especially if you're cooking gluten-free dishes. Here's some advice on how to make these adjustments effectively:

1. Temperature Adjustments:

For most recipes, you can use the same temperature settings in your air fryer as you would in a conventional oven. However, be prepared to check the food for doneness a little earlier than the original recipe's suggested time.

2. Monitoring Cooking Times:

Keep a close eye on your food as it cooks, especially during the first few uses of your air fryer. Cooking times can vary based on the model and wattage.

3. Reduce Cooking Time:

In general, you can reduce the cooking time when using an air fryer compared to traditional methods. Start by decreasing the cooking time by 25% and adjust from there as needed.

4. Shake or Flip Food:

To ensure even cooking, shake the air fryer basket or flip the food halfway through the cooking time. This is particularly important for foods like chicken wings or fries.

5. Adjust for Food Thickness:

Thicker foods may require longer cooking times. Thinly sliced items like potato chips may cook faster than thicker potato wedges. Adjust your cooking times accordingly.

6. Temperature Probe:

Consider using a temperature probe for meats to ensure they reach the desired internal temperature. This prevents overcooking or undercooking.

7. Parchment Paper or Liners:

For items that tend to stick to the basket, use parchment paper or perforated liners. This can help with even cooking and prevent sticking.

8. Test for Doneness:

Invest in a kitchen thermometer to check the internal temperature of meats and ensure they are safe to eat. Different meats have different safe temperatures.

9. Experiment and Document:

Keep a cooking journal where you document the adjustments you make to recipes and the results. This helps refine your air frying technique over time.

10. Air Fryer Manual:

Consult your specific air fryer's manual for guidelines and recommendations on adjusting cooking times and temperatures. Manufacturers often provide useful information.

11. Account for Food Moisture:

Gluten-free recipes may require adjustments due to the moisture content of gluten-free flours. Some dishes may need additional moisture or binding agents to achieve the right texture.

12. Practice and Patience:

The more you use your air fryer, the better you'll become at making adjustments. Practice and patience are key to mastering this cooking method.

Remember that adjusting recipes and cooking times is often a matter of experimentation and practice. Over time, you'll develop a good sense of how your specific air fryer model works and what adjustments are needed for your favorite recipes, including those for gluten-free meals.

TIPS AND TRICKS FOR SUCCESSFUL GLUTEN-FREE AIR FRYING.

Successful gluten-free air frying requires attention to detail and some specific tips and tricks to ensure your dishes turn out delicious and safe for those with gluten sensitivities. Here are some helpful tips:

• Use Certified Gluten-Free Ingredients: Always choose ingredients that are labeled as "gluten-free" to reduce the risk of cross-contamination.

• Gluten-Free Flours: When breading or coating foods, opt for gluten-free flours like rice flour, cornstarch, chickpea flour, or a gluten-free all-purpose flour blend. These can create a crispy texture when air frying.

• Experiment with Breadcrumbs: Gluten-free breadcrumbs are available, but you can also make your own by toasting gluten-free bread and blending it into fine crumbs. Use these for coating or breading.

• Preheat Your Air Fryer: Preheating the air fryer for a few minutes can help ensure even cooking and a crispy texture for your gluten-free dishes.

- Shake Off Excess Flour: After coating food with gluten-free flour, make sure to shake off any excess to prevent a gummy texture.

- Avoid Wet Batters: When frying, avoid wet batters that are high in moisture, as they may not get as crispy as desired. Opt for drier coatings or use gluten-free panko breadcrumbs.

- Use Gluten-Free Sauces and Condiments: Be cautious with sauces and condiments, as some may contain hidden sources of gluten. Look for certified gluten-free options or make your own from scratch.

- Check for Cross-Contamination: Ensure that your air fryer is clean and free of gluten residue before using it for gluten-free cooking. Even small traces of gluten can cause issues.

- Invest in Gluten-Free Cookware: Consider dedicated gluten-free kitchen tools to minimize the risk of cross-contamination. Use separate utensils, cutting boards, and containers for gluten-free cooking.

- Rotate or Flip Food: For even cooking and browning, rotate or flip the food halfway through the cooking time. This is particularly important when air frying breaded items.

• Monitor Cooking Times: Gluten-free dishes may cook faster or slower than their gluten-containing counterparts. Keep a close eye on your food and check for doneness.

• Get Creative: Experiment with gluten-free seasonings, herbs, and spices to add depth and flavor to your dishes. The right seasonings can compensate for the absence of gluten.

• Educate Your Household: If you live with others, educate them about the importance of avoiding cross-contamination when preparing gluten-free meals.

• Keep an Eye on Texture: Achieving the desired texture can be challenging with gluten-free cooking. Experiment with different flours, binders (like xanthan gum or psyllium husk), and techniques to achieve the right texture.

By following these tips and tricks, you can enjoy successful and safe gluten-free air frying while still achieving delicious results. Gluten-free cooking in an air fryer can be a rewarding and tasty experience with the right approach and attention to detail.

CHAPTER TWO

RECIPES

Gluten-Free Air-Fried Chicken Tenders

Ingredients:

- Chicken tenders

- Gluten-free all-purpose flour or rice flour

- Eggs (or a dairy-free alternative)

- Gluten-free breadcrumbs or crushed rice cereal

- Salt, pepper, and your favorite seasonings

Instructions:

1. Dredge the chicken tenders in flour, dip in beaten eggs, and coat with gluten-free breadcrumbs.

2. Preheat your air fryer and lightly grease the basket.

3. Arrange the chicken tenders in a single layer and air fry at 375°F (190°C) for 15-18 minutes, flipping halfway through.

Crispy Air-Fried Gluten-Free Onion Rings

Ingredients:

- Large sweet onions

- Gluten-free all-purpose flour

- Eggs (or a dairy-free alternative)

- Gluten-free breadcrumbs

- Salt, paprika, and cayenne pepper

Instructions:

1. Slice the onions into rings and separate them.

2. Dredge the onion rings in flour, dip in beaten eggs, and coat with seasoned gluten-free breadcrumbs.

3. Preheat the air fryer and arrange the onion rings in a single layer.

4. Air fry at 375°F (190°C) for 10-12 minutes, or until golden brown.

Gluten-Free Air-Fried Sweet Potato Fries

Ingredients:

- Sweet potatoes, peeled and cut into fries
- Olive oil
- Gluten-free cornstarch
- Salt, pepper, and your preferred seasonings

Instructions:

1. Toss the sweet potato fries in a mixture of olive oil and cornstarch to coat them evenly.

2. Preheat the air fryer, and air fry the sweet potato fries at 375°F (190°C) for 15-20 minutes, shaking the basket occasionally until they're crispy.

Air-Fried Gluten-Free Salmon with Herb Crust

Ingredients:

- Salmon fillets
- Gluten-free breadcrumbs or almond flour

- Fresh herbs (e.g., parsley, dill, chives)

- Lemon zest

- Olive oil

- Salt and pepper

Instructions:

1. In a bowl, combine breadcrumbs, finely chopped fresh herbs, lemon zest, olive oil, salt, and pepper.

2. Coat the salmon fillets with the herb mixture.

3. Preheat the air fryer and air fry the salmon at 375°F (190°C) for 10-12 minutes, or until the fish flakes easily.

Gluten-Free Air-Fried Veggie Spring Rolls

Ingredients:

- Gluten-free spring roll wrappers

- Shredded carrots

- Cabbage

- Rice vermicelli noodles (cooked and cooled)

- Cooked shrimp, chicken, or tofu (optional)

- Gluten-free tamari or soy sauce

Instructions:

1. Prepare the spring roll filling by combining shredded veggies, cooked noodles, and your choice of protein.

2. Dip a spring roll wrapper into warm water to soften, then fill it with the mixture.

3. Fold the sides and roll up the wrapper tightly.

4. Preheat the air fryer and lightly spray the spring rolls with oil.

5. Air fry at 375°F (190°C) for 8-10 minutes, turning halfway through until they're crispy.

Gluten-Free Air-Fried Coconut Shrimp

Ingredients:

- Large shrimp, peeled and deveined

- Shredded coconut (unsweetened)

- Eggs (or a dairy-free alternative)

- Gluten-free all-purpose flour

- Salt, pepper, and paprika

Instructions:

1. Dredge the shrimp in flour, dip in beaten eggs, and coat with shredded coconut seasoned with salt, pepper, and paprika.

2. Preheat the air fryer and lightly grease the basket.

3. Arrange the coconut shrimp in a single layer and air fry at 375°F (190°C) for 5-7 minutes, flipping halfway through.

Gluten-Free Air-Fried Avocado Fries

Ingredients:

- Ripe avocados, sliced into fries

- Gluten-free breadcrumbs or almond flour

- Eggs (or a dairy-free alternative)

- Salt, paprika, and cumin

Instructions:

1. Dredge the avocado fries in breadcrumbs or almond flour, dip in beaten eggs, and season with salt, paprika, and cumin.

2. Preheat the air fryer and lightly grease the basket.

3. Arrange the avocado fries in a single layer and air fry at 375°F (190°C) for 8-10 minutes, or until crispy.

Air-Fried Gluten-Free Chicken and Vegetable Skewers

Ingredients:

- Chicken breast or thigh pieces

- Bell peppers, onions, and zucchini, cut into chunks

- Gluten-free marinade (e.g., garlic, lemon, herbs, and olive oil)

Instructions:

1. Marinate the chicken and vegetables in the gluten-free marinade for at least 30 minutes.

2. Thread the marinated chicken and vegetables onto skewers.

3. Preheat the air fryer and air fry the skewers at 375°F (190°C) for 10-15 minutes, turning occasionally until the chicken is cooked through and the vegetables are tender.

Gluten-Free Air-Fried Quinoa-Stuffed Peppers

Ingredients:

- Bell peppers, halved and seeds removed

- Cooked quinoa

- Ground meat (e.g., beef, turkey, or plant-based protein for a vegetarian option)

- Gluten-free tomato sauce

- Seasonings (e.g., garlic, basil, and oregano)

Instructions:

1. In a bowl, mix cooked quinoa, browned ground meat, gluten-free tomato sauce, and seasonings.

2. Fill the halved peppers with the quinoa mixture.

3. Preheat the air fryer and air fry the stuffed peppers at 375°F (190°C) for 15-20 minutes, or until the peppers are tender and the filling is heated through.

Gluten-Free Air-Fried Zucchini Chips

Ingredients:

- Zucchini, thinly sliced

- Gluten-free rice flour or chickpea flour

- Eggs (or a dairy-free alternative)

- Gluten-free breadcrumbs

- Parmesan cheese (optional)

Instructions:

1. Dredge the zucchini slices in flour, dip in beaten eggs, and coat with a mixture of gluten-free breadcrumbs and Parmesan cheese.

2. Preheat the air fryer and lightly grease the basket.

3. Arrange the zucchini slices in a single layer and air fry at 375°F (190°C) for 10-12 minutes, turning once, until they're crisp.

Gluten-Free Air-Fried Vegetable Fritters

Ingredients:

- Grated zucchini, carrots, and potatoes

- Gluten-free chickpea flour or rice flour

- Eggs (or a dairy-free alternative)

- Finely chopped fresh herbs (e.g., parsley and chives)

- Salt and pepper

Instructions:

1. Mix the grated vegetables, flour, eggs, herbs, salt, and pepper in a bowl.

2. Preheat the air fryer and lightly grease the basket.

3. Form the mixture into fritters and place them in the air fryer. Air fry at 375°F (190°C) for 12-15 minutes, turning once, until they're golden and crispy.

Gluten-Free Air-Fried Stuffed Mushrooms

Ingredients:

- Large mushroom caps

- Gluten-free breadcrumbs or almond flour

- Cream cheese (or a dairy-free alternative)

- Fresh garlic, herbs, and grated Parmesan (optional)

Instructions:

1. Remove the stems from the mushroom caps and set them aside.

2. In a bowl, combine cream cheese, gluten-free breadcrumbs, garlic, herbs, and Parmesan (if using).

3. Fill the mushroom caps with the cream cheese mixture.

4. Preheat the air fryer and air fry the stuffed mushrooms at 375°F (190°C) for 10-12 minutes, or until they're tender and lightly browned.

Gluten-Free Air-Fried Eggplant Parmesan

Ingredients:

- Sliced eggplant rounds

- Gluten-free breadcrumbs or almond flour

- Eggs (or a dairy-free alternative)

- Marinara sauce (check for gluten-free)

- Dairy-free mozzarella cheese (or regular mozzarella if tolerated)

Instructions:

1. Dredge the eggplant slices in eggs and coat with gluten-free breadcrumbs.

2. Preheat the air fryer and lightly grease the basket.

3. Arrange the breaded eggplant slices in a single layer and air fry at 375°F (190°C) for 10-12 minutes.

4. Top with marinara sauce and mozzarella, then air fry for an additional 3-4 minutes, or until the cheese is melted and bubbly.

Gluten-Free Air-Fried Tofu with Peanut Sauce

Ingredients:

- Cubed extra-firm tofu

- Gluten-free cornstarch

- Salt and pepper

- Gluten-free peanut sauce (store-bought or homemade)

Instructions:

1. Toss the tofu cubes in cornstarch, salt, and pepper.

2. Preheat the air fryer and lightly grease the basket.

3. Arrange the tofu cubes in a single layer and air fry at 375°F (190°C) for 15-20 minutes, turning occasionally until they're crispy.

4. Serve with gluten-free peanut sauce for dipping.

Gluten-Free Air-Fried Banana Fritters

Ingredients:

- Ripe bananas, sliced into rounds

- Gluten-free rice flour or chickpea flour

- Cinnamon and sugar (or a sugar substitute)

- Cooking oil spray

Instructions:

1. In a bowl, coat the banana slices in flour mixed with cinnamon and sugar.

2. Preheat the air fryer and lightly grease the basket.

3. Arrange the banana slices in a single layer and air fry at 375°F (190°C) for 5-6 minutes, turning once, until they're golden and crispy.

Gluten-Free Air-Fried Calamari Rings

Ingredients:

- Calamari rings (fresh or frozen)

- Gluten-free rice flour

- Paprika and garlic powder

- Lemon wedges for serving

Instructions:

1. Toss the calamari rings in gluten-free rice flour seasoned with paprika and garlic powder.

2. Preheat the air fryer and lightly grease the basket.

3. Arrange the coated calamari rings in a single layer and air fry at 375°F (190°C) for 5-7 minutes, or until they're crispy and golden. Serve with lemon wedges.

Gluten-Free Air-Fried Shrimp Tacos

Ingredients:

- Large shrimp, peeled and deveined
- Gluten-free taco seasoning
- Corn tortillas
- Sliced cabbage, salsa, and lime wedges for toppings

Instructions:

1. Season the shrimp with gluten-free taco seasoning.

2. Preheat the air fryer and lightly grease the basket.

3. Arrange the shrimp in a single layer and air fry at 375°F (190°C) for 6-8 minutes, turning once, until they're cooked through.

4. Serve the shrimp in corn tortillas with sliced cabbage, salsa, and lime wedges.

Gluten-Free Air-Fried Mac and Cheese Bites

Ingredients:

- Gluten-free mac and cheese (cooked and cooled)

- Gluten-free breadcrumbs or almond flour

- Eggs (or a dairy-free alternative)

Instructions:

1. Roll the chilled mac and cheese into bite-sized balls.

2. Dip the mac and cheese bites in beaten eggs and coat with gluten-free breadcrumbs or almond flour.

3. Preheat the air fryer and lightly grease the basket.

4. Arrange the mac and cheese bites in a single layer and air fry at 375°F (190°C) for 8-10 minutes, or until they're crispy and golden.

Gluten-Free Air-Fried Stuffed Peppers

Ingredients:

- Bell peppers, tops removed and seeds removed

- Gluten-free cooked rice

- Ground meat or plant-based protein

- Gluten-free tomato sauce

- Seasonings (e.g., garlic, basil, and oregano)

Instructions:

1. In a bowl, combine cooked rice, browned ground meat or plant-based protein, gluten-free tomato sauce, and seasonings.

2. Fill the bell peppers with the mixture.

3. Preheat the air fryer and air fry the stuffed peppers at 375°F (190°C) for 20-25 minutes, or until the peppers are tender and the filling is heated through.

Gluten-Free Air-Fried Apple Cinnamon Donuts

Ingredients:

- Gluten-free donut mix (prepare according to package instructions)

- Chopped apples

- Cinnamon and sugar (or a sugar substitute)

Instructions:

1. Mix the gluten-free donut batter and fold in the chopped apples.

2. Preheat the air fryer and lightly grease the basket.

3. Spoon the batter into donut molds and air fry at 350°F (175°C) for 8-10 minutes or until they're golden and cooked through.

4. While still warm, sprinkle with a mixture of cinnamon and sugar.

Gluten-Free Air-Fried Buffalo Cauliflower Bites

Ingredients:

- Cauliflower florets

- Gluten-free rice flour or chickpea flour

- Buffalo hot sauce (check for gluten-free)

- Garlic powder and paprika

Instructions:

1. Toss cauliflower florets in gluten-free flour mixed with garlic powder and paprika.

2. Preheat the air fryer and lightly grease the basket.

3. Arrange the coated cauliflower in a single layer and air fry at 375°F (190°C) for 15-18 minutes.

4. Toss the cooked cauliflower in buffalo hot sauce and air fry for an additional 2-3 minutes. Serve with celery and ranch (check for gluten-free) or blue cheese dressing.

Gluten-Free Air-Fried Beef and Vegetable Stir-Fry

Ingredients:

- Thinly sliced beef strips

- Sliced bell peppers, broccoli, and snap peas

- Gluten-free stir-fry sauce (check for gluten-free)

- Cooked rice or rice noodles

Instructions:

1. Stir-fry the beef and vegetables in a pan with gluten-free stir-fry sauce until cooked.

2. Preheat the air fryer and warm the cooked rice or rice noodles.

3. Serve the beef and vegetable stir-fry over the rice or noodles. Garnish with sesame seeds or green onions.

Gluten-Free Air-Fried Stuffed Mushrooms with Spinach and Cheese

Ingredients:

- Large mushroom caps

- Fresh spinach, chopped

- Gluten-free cream cheese

- Grated Parmesan cheese

- Garlic and onion powder

Instructions:

1. Remove the stems from the mushroom caps and set them aside.

2. In a bowl, mix chopped spinach, gluten-free cream cheese, grated Parmesan, garlic and onion powder, and the mushroom stems.

3. Fill the mushroom caps with the spinach and cheese mixture.

4. Preheat the air fryer and air fry the stuffed mushrooms at 375°F (190°C) for 12-15 minutes, or until they're tender and the filling is heated through.

Gluten-Free Air-Fried Fish Tacos

Ingredients:

- White fish fillets (e.g., cod or tilapia)

- Gluten-free corn tortillas

- Cabbage slaw (cabbage, carrots, and gluten-free coleslaw dressing)

- Fresh cilantro and lime wedges

Instructions:

1. Season the fish fillets with your preferred gluten-free seasonings.

2. Preheat the air fryer and lightly grease the basket.

3. Arrange the fish fillets in a single layer and air fry at 375°F (190°C) for 10-12 minutes, or until the fish is cooked through and crispy.

4. Assemble fish tacos in corn tortillas with cabbage slaw, fresh cilantro, and lime wedges.

Gluten-Free Air-Fried Chocolate Brownie Bites

Ingredients:

- Gluten-free brownie mix (prepare according to package instructions)

- Mini muffin paper liners

Instructions:

1. Prepare the gluten-free brownie mix.

2. Line the air fryer basket with mini muffin paper liners and spoon the brownie mixture into each liner.

3. Preheat the air fryer and air fry the brownie bites at 350°F (175°C) for 8-10 minutes, or until they're baked through. Let them cool before serving.

Gluten-Free Air-Fried Zesty Lemon Chicken

Ingredients:

- Chicken thighs or breasts

- Gluten-free lemon pepper seasoning

- Olive oil

- Lemon wedges

Instructions:

1. Season the chicken with gluten-free lemon pepper seasoning and a drizzle of olive oil.

2. Preheat the air fryer and lightly grease the basket.

3. Arrange the chicken pieces in a single layer and air fry at 375°F (190°C) for 20-25 minutes or until the chicken reaches a safe internal temperature. Serve with lemon wedges.

Gluten-Free Air-Fried Stuffed Bell Peppers with Quinoa and Black Beans

Ingredients:

- Bell peppers, tops removed and seeds removed
- Cooked quinoa
- Cooked black beans
- Gluten-free tomato sauce
- Chili powder and cumin

Instructions:

1. In a bowl, combine cooked quinoa, black beans, gluten-free tomato sauce, and seasonings.

2. Fill the bell peppers with the quinoa and black bean mixture.

3. Preheat the air fryer and air fry the stuffed peppers at 375°F (190°C) for 20-25 minutes, or until the peppers are tender and the filling is heated through.

Gluten-Free Air-Fried Stuffed Apples with Cinnamon and Pecans

Ingredients:

- Apples, cored and halved

- Gluten-free rolled oats

- Chopped pecans

- Cinnamon and a drizzle of maple syrup

Instructions:

1. Mix gluten-free rolled oats, chopped pecans, cinnamon, and a drizzle of maple syrup.

2. Fill the apple halves with the oat and pecan mixture.

3. Preheat the air fryer and air fry the stuffed apples at 350°F (175°C) for 10-12 minutes, or until they're tender and lightly browned.

Gluten-Free Air-Fried Garlic Herb Shrimp Skewers

Ingredients:

- Large shrimp, peeled and deveined

- Olive oil

- Chopped fresh herbs (e.g., parsley, thyme, and rosemary)

- Minced garlic

Instructions:

1. Marinate the shrimp in a mixture of olive oil, chopped herbs, and minced garlic for about 20 minutes.

2. Thread the marinated shrimp onto skewers.

3. Preheat the air fryer and air fry the shrimp skewers at 375°F (190°C) for 5-7 minutes, turning once, until they're pink and cooked through.

Gluten-Free Air-Fried Stuffed Tomatoes with Quinoa and Feta

Ingredients:

- Large tomatoes, tops removed and seeds removed

- Cooked quinoa

- Crumbled feta cheese

- Fresh basil leaves

- Balsamic glaze (check for gluten-free)

Instructions:

1. In a bowl, combine cooked quinoa, crumbled feta cheese, and fresh basil leaves.

2. Fill the tomatoes with the quinoa and feta mixture.

3. Preheat the air fryer and air fry the stuffed tomatoes at 375°F (190°C) for 12-15 minutes, or until the tomatoes are tender and the filling is heated through.

4. Drizzle with balsamic glaze before serving.

Gluten-Free Air-Fried Coconut Crusted Tilapia

Ingredients:

- Tilapia fillets

- Gluten-free shredded coconut

- Gluten-free rice flour

- Eggs (or a dairy-free alternative)

Instructions:

1. Dredge the tilapia fillets in rice flour, dip in beaten eggs, and coat with shredded coconut.

2. Preheat the air fryer and lightly grease the basket.

3. Arrange the coated tilapia in a single layer and air fry at 375°F (190°C) for 10-12 minutes or until the fish is cooked through and the coconut is golden and crispy.

Gluten-Free Air-Fried Sweet Chili Chicken Wings

Ingredients:

- Chicken wings

- Gluten-free sweet chili sauce (check for gluten-free)

- Salt and pepper

Instructions:

1. Season the chicken wings with salt and pepper.

2. Preheat the air fryer and lightly grease the basket.

3. Arrange the chicken wings in a single layer and air fry at 375°F (190°C) for 25-30 minutes, turning once, until they're crispy.

4. Toss the wings in sweet chili sauce before serving.

Gluten-Free Air-Fried Asparagus with Parmesan

Ingredients:

- Fresh asparagus spears

- Olive oil

- Grated Parmesan cheese

- Garlic powder

Instructions:

1. Toss the asparagus spears in olive oil and sprinkle with grated Parmesan and garlic powder.

2. Preheat the air fryer and lightly grease the basket.

3. Arrange the asparagus in a single layer and air fry at 375°F (190°C) for 8-10 minutes or until they're tender and the cheese is golden and bubbly.

Gluten-Free Air-Fried Stuffed Bell Peppers with Rice and Ground Turkey

Ingredients:

- Bell peppers, tops removed and seeds removed

- Cooked gluten-free rice

- Cooked ground turkey (seasoned with your choice of gluten-free spices)

- Gluten-free tomato sauce

Instructions:

1. In a bowl, combine cooked rice, seasoned ground turkey, and gluten-free tomato sauce.

2. Fill the bell peppers with the rice and turkey mixture.

3. Preheat the air fryer and air fry the stuffed peppers at 375°F (190°C) for 20-25 minutes, or until the peppers are tender and the filling is heated through.

Gluten-Free Air-Fried Cheesy Garlic Breadsticks

Ingredients:

• Gluten-free pizza dough or breadstick dough (prepared according to package instructions)

• Olive oil

• Garlic powder and dried basil

• Shredded mozzarella cheese

Instructions:

1. Roll out the gluten-free pizza dough into breadsticks.

2. Brush the breadsticks with olive oil and sprinkle with garlic powder, dried basil, and shredded mozzarella cheese.

3. Preheat the air fryer and air fry the breadsticks at 375°F (190°C) for 10-12 minutes or until they're golden and the cheese is melted.

Gluten-Free Air-Fried Stuffed Portobello Mushrooms

Ingredients:

- Large Portobello mushrooms, stems removed
- Gluten-free Italian-style breadcrumbs
- Cooked and crumbled gluten-free Italian sausage
- Chopped fresh parsley
- Grated Parmesan cheese

Instructions:

1. In a bowl, mix gluten-free breadcrumbs, crumbled Italian sausage, chopped parsley, and grated Parmesan.

2. Fill the Portobello mushrooms with the breadcrumb mixture.

3. Preheat the air fryer and air fry the stuffed mushrooms at 375°F (190°C) for 12-15 minutes, or until the mushrooms are tender and the filling is heated through.

Gluten-Free Air-Fried Thai Basil Tofu

Ingredients:

- Extra-firm tofu, cubed

- Gluten-free cornstarch

- Thai basil leaves

- Gluten-free Thai basil sauce (check for gluten-free)

Instructions:

1. Toss the tofu cubes in gluten-free cornstarch to coat.

2. Preheat the air fryer and lightly grease the basket.

3. Arrange the tofu in a single layer and air fry at 375°F (190°C) for 15-20 minutes, turning occasionally until they're crispy.

4. Toss the crispy tofu with Thai basil sauce and fresh basil leaves before serving.

Gluten-Free Air-Fried Brussel Sprouts with Balsamic Glaze

Ingredients:

- Brussel sprouts, trimmed and halved

- Olive oil

- Balsamic glaze (check for gluten-free)

- Salt and pepper

Instructions:

1. Toss the Brussel sprouts in olive oil, salt, and pepper.

2. Preheat the air fryer and lightly grease the basket.

3. Arrange the Brussel sprouts in a single layer and air fry at 375°F (190°C) for 12-15 minutes or until they're crispy and caramelized.

4. Drizzle with balsamic glaze before serving.

Gluten-Free Air-Fried Chicken Parmesan

Ingredients:

- Chicken breast cutlets

- Gluten-free breadcrumbs

- Eggs (or a dairy-free alternative)

- Marinara sauce (check for gluten-free)

- Shredded mozzarella cheese

Instructions:

1. Dredge the chicken cutlets in beaten eggs and coat with gluten-free breadcrumbs.

2. Preheat the air fryer and lightly grease the basket.

3. Arrange the breaded chicken cutlets in a single layer and air fry at 375°F (190°C) for 15-18 minutes or until they're cooked through and crispy.

4. Top with marinara sauce and mozzarella cheese, then air fry for an additional 3-4 minutes until the cheese is melted and bubbly.

Gluten-Free Air-Fried Banana and Blueberry Muffins

Ingredients:

- Gluten-free muffin mix (prepared according to package instructions)

- Ripe mashed bananas

- Fresh blueberries

- Cinnamon and sugar (or a sugar substitute)

Instructions:

1. Prepare the gluten-free muffin mix and fold in mashed bananas and fresh blueberries.

2. Fill muffin cups with the batter and sprinkle with cinnamon and sugar.

3. Preheat the air fryer and air fry the muffins at 350°F (175°C) for 12-15 minutes, or until they're baked through.

Gluten-Free Air-Fried Mozzarella Sticks

Ingredients:

- Gluten-free mozzarella cheese sticks

- Gluten-free breadcrumbs or almond flour

- Eggs (or a dairy-free alternative)

- Marinara sauce (check for gluten-free)

Instructions:

1. Dredge the mozzarella sticks in beaten eggs and coat with gluten-free breadcrumbs or almond flour.

2. Preheat the air fryer and lightly grease the basket.

3. Arrange the coated mozzarella sticks in a single layer and air fry at 375°F (190°C) for 5-7 minutes or until they're golden and the cheese is melted. Serve with marinara sauce for dipping.

Gluten-Free Air-Fried Stuffed Acorn Squash

Ingredients:

- Acorn squash, halved and seeds removed

- Cooked quinoa

- Cooked ground sausage or a meatless alternative

- Diced apples and cranberries

- Cinnamon and nutmeg

Instructions:

1. In a bowl, mix cooked quinoa, cooked sausage or meatless alternative, diced apples, cranberries, and a sprinkle of cinnamon and nutmeg.

2. Fill the acorn squash halves with the quinoa mixture.

3. Preheat the air fryer and air fry the stuffed acorn squash at 375°F (190°C) for 20-25 minutes or until the squash is tender and the filling is heated through.

Gluten-Free Air-Fried Ratatouille

Ingredients:

- Sliced zucchini, eggplant, and bell peppers

- Sliced tomatoes

- Chopped onions and garlic

- Olive oil

- Fresh basil and thyme

Instructions:

1. Toss the sliced vegetables, onions, and garlic in olive oil and fresh herbs.

2. Preheat the air fryer and lightly grease the basket.

3. Arrange the seasoned vegetables in the air fryer and air fry at 375°F (190°C) for 20-25 minutes or until they're tender and slightly caramelized.

Gluten-Free Air-Fried Chocolate-Covered Strawberries

Ingredients:

- Fresh strawberries

- Gluten-free dark chocolate, melted

- Chopped nuts or shredded coconut (optional)

Instructions:

1. Dip the strawberries in melted gluten-free dark chocolate.

2. Optionally, roll them in chopped nuts or shredded coconut for added texture.

3. Place the chocolate-covered strawberries in the air fryer basket.

4. Preheat the air fryer and air fry at 350°F (175°C) for 2-3 minutes until the chocolate is set.

Gluten-Free Air-Fried Stuffed Bell Peppers with Rice and Black Beans

Ingredients:

- Bell peppers, tops removed and seeds removed

- Cooked gluten-free rice

- Cooked black beans

- Gluten-free tomato sauce

Instructions:

1. In a bowl, combine cooked rice, black beans, and gluten-free tomato sauce.

2. Fill the bell peppers with the rice and black bean mixture.

3. Preheat the air fryer and air fry the stuffed peppers at 375°F (190°C) for 20-25 minutes or until the peppers are tender and the filling is heated through.

Gluten-Free Air-Fried Sweet Potato Fries

Ingredients:

- Sweet potatoes, cut into fries

- Olive oil

- Gluten-free paprika and garlic powder

Instructions:

1. Toss the sweet potato fries in olive oil and season with gluten-free paprika and garlic powder.

2. Preheat the air fryer and lightly grease the basket.

3. Arrange the seasoned sweet potato fries in a single layer and air fry at 375°F (190°C) for 15-20 minutes or until they're crispy and golden.

Gluten-Free Air-Fried Stuffed Mushrooms with Spinach and Bacon

Ingredients:

- Large mushroom caps

- Fresh spinach, chopped

- Cooked and crumbled gluten-free bacon

- Cream cheese (or a dairy-free alternative)

Instructions:

1. Remove the stems from the mushroom caps and set them aside.

2. In a bowl, mix chopped spinach, crumbled bacon, and cream cheese.

3. Fill the mushroom caps with the spinach and bacon mixture.

4. Preheat the air fryer and air fry the stuffed mushrooms at 375°F (190°C) for 12-15 minutes, or until they're tender and the filling is heated through.

Gluten-Free Air-Fried Chicken Tenders with Honey Mustard Sauce

Ingredients:

- Chicken tenders

- Gluten-free breadcrumbs or almond flour

- Eggs (or a dairy-free alternative)

- Honey mustard sauce (check for gluten-free)

Instructions:

1. Dredge the chicken tenders in eggs and coat with gluten-free breadcrumbs or almond flour.

2. Preheat the air fryer and lightly grease the basket.

3. Arrange the coated chicken tenders in a single layer and air fry at 375°F (190°C) for 12-15 minutes or until they're crispy and cooked through.

4. Serve with gluten-free honey mustard sauce for dipping.

Gluten-Free Air-Fried Cinnamon Sugar Apple Chips

Ingredients:

- Apples, thinly sliced

- Cinnamon and sugar (or a sugar substitute)

Instructions:

1. Toss the apple slices in cinnamon and sugar.

2. Preheat the air fryer and lightly grease the basket.

3. Arrange the seasoned apple slices in a single layer and air fry at 350°F (175°C) for 10-12 minutes or until they're crispy and golden.

Gluten-Free Air-Fried Shrimp Po' Boy Sandwich

Ingredients:

- Gluten-free bread or rolls

- Large shrimp, peeled and deveined

- Gluten-free cornmeal

- Eggs (or a dairy-free alternative)

• Shredded lettuce, sliced tomatoes, and gluten-free remoulade sauce

Instructions:

1. Coat the shrimp in gluten-free cornmeal and dip in beaten eggs.

2. Preheat the air fryer and lightly grease the basket.

3. Arrange the coated shrimp in a single layer and air fry at 375°F (190°C) for 5-7 minutes or until they're crispy and cooked through.

4. Assemble the shrimp, lettuce, tomatoes, and remoulade sauce in gluten-free bread or rolls for a delicious Po' Boy sandwich.

Gluten-Free Air-Fried Stuffed Avocado with Quinoa and Salsa

Ingredients:

• Ripe avocados, halved and pitted

• Cooked quinoa

• Gluten-free salsa

- Fresh cilantro and lime wedges

Instructions:

1. In a bowl, mix cooked quinoa and salsa.

2. Fill the avocado halves with the quinoa and salsa mixture.

3. Preheat the air fryer and air fry the stuffed avocados at 375°F (190°C) for 8-10 minutes or until they're heated through.

4. Garnish with fresh cilantro and serve with lime wedges.

Gluten-Free Air-Fried Stuffed Eggplant with Italian Sausage and Cheese

Ingredients:

- Eggplants, halved and scooped out

- Cooked gluten-free Italian sausage

- Grated mozzarella and Parmesan cheese

- Gluten-free tomato sauce

Instructions:

1. Mix cooked Italian sausage, grated cheese, and gluten-free tomato sauce.

2. Fill the eggplant halves with the sausage and cheese mixture.

3. Preheat the air fryer and air fry the stuffed eggplants at 375°F (190°C) for 15-18 minutes or until they're tender and the filling is heated through.

Gluten-Free Air-Fried Potato Latkes

Ingredients:

- Russet potatoes, peeled and grated

- Finely grated onion

- Eggs (or a dairy-free alternative)

- Gluten-free potato starch or cornstarch

- Salt and pepper

Instructions:

1. Mix grated potatoes, finely grated onion, eggs, potato starch, salt, and pepper in a bowl.

2. Preheat the air fryer and lightly grease the basket.

3. Form the potato mixture into latkes and arrange them in a single layer.

4. Air fry at 375°F (190°C) for 8-10 minutes per side, or until they're crispy and golden.

Gluten-Free Air-Fried Pineapple and Shrimp Skewers

Ingredients:

- Large shrimp, peeled and deveined

- Pineapple chunks

- Gluten-free teriyaki sauce (check for gluten-free)

- Bell peppers and red onion chunks

Instructions:

1. Thread the shrimp, pineapple, bell peppers, and red onion onto skewers.

2. Brush the skewers with gluten-free teriyaki sauce.

3. Preheat the air fryer and air fry the skewers at 375°F (190°C) for 8-10 minutes, turning once, until the shrimp are pink and cooked through.

Gluten-Free Air-Fried Green Bean Fries

Ingredients:

- Fresh green beans, washed and trimmed

- Gluten-free breadcrumbs or almond flour

- Eggs (or a dairy-free alternative)

- Gluten-free ranch dressing (check for gluten-free)

Instructions:

1. Dip the green beans in beaten eggs and coat with gluten-free breadcrumbs or almond flour.

2. Preheat the air fryer and lightly grease the basket.

3. Arrange the coated green beans in a single layer and air fry at 375°F (190°C) for 10-12 minutes or until they're crispy and tender. Serve with gluten-free ranch dressing for dipping.

Gluten-Free Air-Fried Stuffed Bell Peppers with Quinoa and Vegetables

Ingredients:

- Bell peppers, tops removed and seeds removed

- Cooked quinoa

- Sautéed mixed vegetables (e.g., bell peppers, corn, and zucchini)

- Gluten-free tomato sauce

Instructions:

1. In a bowl, combine cooked quinoa, sautéed vegetables, and gluten-free tomato sauce.

2. Fill the bell peppers with the quinoa and vegetable mixture.

3. Preheat the air fryer and air fry the stuffed peppers at 375°F (190°C) for 20-25 minutes or until the peppers are tender and the filling is heated through.

Gluten-Free Air-Fried Garlic Herb Hasselback Potatoes

Ingredients:

- Small potatoes, thinly sliced but not all the way through

- Olive oil

- Minced garlic and dried herbs (e.g., rosemary and thyme)

- Salt and pepper

Instructions:

1. Toss the potatoes with olive oil, minced garlic, dried herbs, salt, and pepper.

2. Preheat the air fryer and lightly grease the basket.

3. Arrange the potatoes in a single layer and air fry at 375°F (190°C) for 25-30 minutes or until they're crispy and cooked through.

Gluten-Free Air-Fried BBQ Chicken Drumsticks

Ingredients:

- Chicken drumsticks

- Gluten-free BBQ sauce (check for gluten-free)

- Salt and pepper

Instructions:

1. Season the chicken drumsticks with salt and pepper.

2. Preheat the air fryer and lightly grease the basket.

3. Arrange the drumsticks in a single layer and air fry at 375°F (190°C) for 25-30 minutes, turning occasionally until they're cooked through.

4. Brush with gluten-free BBQ sauce before serving.

Gluten-Free Air-Fried Banana Walnut Bread

Ingredients:

- Gluten-free banana bread batter (prepared according to package instructions)

- Chopped walnuts

Instructions:

1. Prepare the gluten-free banana bread batter and fold in chopped walnuts.

2. Line a loaf pan with parchment paper and pour in the batter.

3. Preheat the air fryer and air fry the banana bread at 320°F (160°C) for 20-25 minutes or until it's baked through.

Gluten-Free Air-Fried Falafel

Ingredients:

- Canned chickpeas, drained and rinsed

- Chopped fresh parsley and cilantro

- Gluten-free ground cumin, coriander, and garlic powder

- Gluten-free chickpea flour

- Olive oil for brushing

Instructions:

1. In a food processor, blend chickpeas, parsley, cilantro, spices, and chickpea flour until a dough forms.

2. Form the dough into small falafel balls and brush with olive oil.

3. Preheat the air fryer and air fry the falafel at 375°F (190°C) for 12-15 minutes, or until they're crispy and cooked through. Serve with gluten-free tzatziki or hummus.

Gluten-Free Air-Fried Stuffed Zucchini Boats

Ingredients:

- Zucchini, halved and scooped out

- Cooked gluten-free quinoa

- Ground turkey or a meatless alternative

- Chopped bell peppers, onions, and tomatoes

- Gluten-free Italian seasoning

Instructions:

1. In a bowl, combine cooked quinoa, cooked ground turkey or meatless alternative, chopped vegetables, and Italian seasoning.

2. Fill the zucchini halves with the quinoa and turkey mixture.

3. Preheat the air fryer and air fry the stuffed zucchini at 375°F (190°C) for 20-25 minutes, or until they're tender and the filling is heated through.

Gluten-Free Air-Fried Teriyaki Tofu and Vegetable Skewers

Ingredients:

- Extra-firm tofu, cubed

- Gluten-free teriyaki sauce (check for gluten-free)

- Sliced bell peppers, zucchini, and red onion

- Skewers

Instructions:

1. Marinate the tofu and vegetables in gluten-free teriyaki sauce for about 30 minutes.

2. Thread the tofu and vegetables onto skewers.

3. Preheat the air fryer and air fry the skewers at 375°F (190°C) for 12-15 minutes, turning occasionally, until they're cooked and slightly charred.

Gluten-Free Air-Fried Stuffed Artichokes

Ingredients:

- Fresh artichokes, trimmed and steamed
- Gluten-free breadcrumbs
- Chopped fresh herbs (e.g., parsley and thyme)
- Minced garlic
- Olive oil

Instructions:

1. In a bowl, mix gluten-free breadcrumbs, herbs, minced garlic, and olive oil.

2. Fill the steamed artichokes with the breadcrumb mixture.

3. Preheat the air fryer and air fry the stuffed artichokes at 375°F (190°C) for 12-15 minutes, or until they're tender and the filling is golden.

Gluten-Free Air-Fried Cinnamon Sugar Donuts

Ingredients:

- Gluten-free donut dough (prepared according to package instructions)

- Cinnamon and sugar (or a sugar substitute)

Instructions:

1. Prepare the gluten-free donut dough and shape into donuts.

2. Coat the donuts in a mixture of cinnamon and sugar.

3. Preheat the air fryer and air fry the donuts at 350°F (175°C) for 8-10 minutes, or until they're golden and baked through.

Gluten-Free Air-Fried Stuffed Bell Peppers with Mexican Rice and Black Beans

Ingredients:

- Bell peppers, tops removed and seeds removed

- Cooked gluten-free Mexican rice

- Cooked black beans

- Chopped tomatoes and corn

- Gluten-free taco seasoning

Instructions:

1. In a bowl, combine cooked Mexican rice, black beans, tomatoes, corn, and taco seasoning.

2. Fill the bell peppers with the rice and bean mixture.

3. Preheat the air fryer and air fry the stuffed peppers at 375°F (190°C) for 20-25 minutes, or until the peppers are tender and the filling is heated through.

Gluten-Free Air-Fried Stuffed Portobello Mushrooms with Spinach and Feta

Ingredients:

- Large Portobello mushrooms, stems removed

- Fresh spinach, chopped

- Crumbled feta cheese

- Minced garlic and olive oil

Instructions:

1. In a pan, sauté chopped spinach with minced garlic and olive oil until wilted.

2. Fill the Portobello mushrooms with sautéed spinach and crumbled feta cheese.

3. Preheat the air fryer and air fry the stuffed mushrooms at 375°F (190°C) for 12-15 minutes, or until they're tender and the filling is heated through.

Gluten-Free Air-Fried Buffalo Cauliflower Bites

Ingredients:

- Cauliflower florets

- Gluten-free rice flour

- Buffalo sauce (check for gluten-free)

- Olive oil

Instructions:

1. Toss the cauliflower florets in rice flour and olive oil.

2. Preheat the air fryer and lightly grease the basket.

3. Arrange the coated cauliflower in a single layer and air fry at 375°F (190°C) for 15-20 minutes or until they're crispy.

4. Toss the cauliflower in gluten-free buffalo sauce before serving.

Gluten-Free Air-Fried Pork Chops

Ingredients:

- Pork chops

- Gluten-free bread crumbs or almond flour

- Eggs (or a dairy-free alternative)

- Gluten-free Italian seasoning

Instructions:

1. Dredge the pork chops in beaten eggs and coat with gluten-free bread crumbs or almond flour mixed with Italian seasoning.

2. Preheat the air fryer and lightly grease the basket.

3. Arrange the coated pork chops in a single layer and air fry at 375°F (190°C) for 12-15 minutes or until they're cooked through and crispy.

Gluten-Free Air-Fried Brussels Sprouts with Bacon

Ingredients:

- Brussels sprouts, trimmed and halved

- Gluten-free bacon, cooked and crumbled

- Olive oil

- Balsamic glaze (check for gluten-free)

Instructions:

1. Toss the Brussels sprouts in olive oil and season with salt and pepper.

2. Preheat the air fryer and lightly grease the basket.

3. Arrange the Brussels sprouts in a single layer and air fry at 375°F (190°C) for 12-15 minutes or until they're crispy and caramelized.

4. Sprinkle the cooked bacon on top and drizzle with balsamic glaze.

Gluten-Free Air-Fried Stuffed Chicken Breasts with Spinach and Sun-Dried Tomatoes

Ingredients:

- Chicken breasts, pounded thin

- Fresh spinach

- Chopped sun-dried tomatoes

- Gluten-free cream cheese (or a dairy-free alternative)

Instructions:

1. Spread a layer of cream cheese on each pounded chicken breast.

2. Top with fresh spinach and sun-dried tomatoes.

3. Roll up the chicken breasts and secure with toothpicks.

4. Preheat the air fryer and air fry the stuffed chicken breasts at 375°F (190°C) for 20-25 minutes or until they're cooked through.

Gluten-Free Air-Fried Cilantro-Lime Shrimp Tacos

Ingredients:

- Large shrimp, peeled and deveined

- Gluten-free taco seasoning

- Fresh cilantro and lime juice

- Corn tortillas (check for gluten-free)

Instructions:

1. Toss the shrimp in gluten-free taco seasoning and squeeze fresh lime juice over them.

2. Preheat the air fryer and lightly grease the basket.

3. Arrange the shrimp in a single layer and air fry at 375°F (190°C) for 5-7 minutes or until they're cooked through.

4. Assemble the shrimp in corn tortillas and garnish with fresh cilantro.

Gluten-Free Air-Fried Chocolate Lava Cakes

Ingredients:

- Gluten-free chocolate cake batter (prepared according to package instructions)

- Gluten-free chocolate chips or chunks

Instructions:

1. Prepare the gluten-free chocolate cake batter and fill ramekins halfway.

2. Place chocolate chips or chunks in the center of each ramekin.

3. Cover with more batter.

4. Preheat the air fryer and air fry the lava cakes at 350°F (175°C) for 10-12 minutes or until they're baked with a molten center.

Gluten-Free Air-Fried Buffalo Cauliflower Tacos

Ingredients:

- Cauliflower florets

- Gluten-free rice flour

- Buffalo sauce (check for gluten-free)

- Corn tortillas (check for gluten-free)

- Shredded lettuce, diced tomatoes, and ranch dressing (check for gluten-free)

Instructions:

1. Toss the cauliflower florets in rice flour and buffalo sauce.

2. Preheat the air fryer and lightly grease the basket.

3. Arrange the coated cauliflower in a single layer and air fry at 375°F (190°C) for 15-20 minutes or until they're crispy.

4. Assemble the cauliflower in corn tortillas with shredded lettuce, diced tomatoes, and a drizzle of gluten-free ranch dressing.

Gluten-Free Air-Fried Zucchini Noodles with Pesto and Cherry Tomatoes

Ingredients:

- Zucchini noodles (zoodles)

- Gluten-free pesto sauce (check for gluten-free)

- Cherry tomatoes, halved

- Pine nuts (optional)

Instructions:

1. Toss the zucchini noodles with gluten-free pesto sauce and cherry tomato halves.

2. Preheat the air fryer and lightly grease the basket.

3. Arrange the zucchini noodles in the air fryer and air fry at 375°F (190°C) for 5-7 minutes, or until they're tender and heated through.

4. Top with pine nuts if desired before serving.

Gluten-Free Air-Fried Stuffed Sweet Potatoes with Chickpeas and Tahini Sauce

Ingredients:

- Sweet potatoes, baked and halved
- Cooked chickpeas
- Gluten-free tahini sauce
- Chopped fresh parsley

Instructions:

1. In a bowl, mix cooked chickpeas with gluten-free tahini sauce.

2. Fill the sweet potato halves with the chickpea mixture.

3. Preheat the air fryer and air fry the stuffed sweet potatoes at 375°F (190°C) for 8-10 minutes or until they're heated through.

4. Garnish with chopped fresh parsley before serving.

Gluten-Free Air-Fried Lemon Pepper Shrimp and Asparagus

Ingredients:

- Large shrimp, peeled and deveined

- Fresh asparagus spears

- Olive oil

- Lemon pepper seasoning (check for gluten-free)

Instructions:

1. Toss the shrimp and asparagus in olive oil and season with lemon pepper.

2. Preheat the air fryer and lightly grease the basket.

3. Arrange the shrimp and asparagus in a single layer and air fry at 375°F (190°C) for 8-10 minutes or until the shrimp are pink and cooked through.

Gluten-Free Air-Fried Coconut Chicken Tenders

Ingredients:

- Chicken tenders

- Gluten-free shredded coconut

- Gluten-free coconut milk

- Gluten-free rice flour

Instructions:

1. Dip the chicken tenders in gluten-free rice flour and coat with a mixture of shredded coconut and coconut milk.

2. Preheat the air fryer and lightly grease the basket.

3. Arrange the coated chicken tenders in a single layer and air fry at 375°F (190°C) for 12-15 minutes or until they're crispy and cooked through.

4. Serve with your favorite gluten-free dipping sauce.

Gluten-Free Air-Fried Stuffed Mushrooms with Crab and Cream Cheese

Ingredients:

- Large mushroom caps

- Gluten-free cream cheese

- Cooked crab meat

- Chopped fresh parsley and paprika

Instructions:

1. In a bowl, mix cream cheese, crab meat, parsley, and paprika.

2. Fill the mushroom caps with the cream cheese and crab mixture.

3. Preheat the air fryer and air fry the stuffed mushrooms at 375°F (190°C) for 12-15 minutes, or until they're tender and heated through.

Gluten-Free Air-Fried Mozzarella Sticks

Ingredients:

- Gluten-free mozzarella string cheese sticks

- Gluten-free breadcrumbs

- Eggs (or a dairy-free alternative)

- Marinara sauce (check for gluten-free)

Instructions:

1. Cut the mozzarella sticks in half.

2. Dip each stick in beaten eggs and coat with gluten-free breadcrumbs.

3. Preheat the air fryer and lightly grease the basket.

4. Arrange the coated mozzarella sticks in a single layer and air fry at 375°F (190°C) for 6-8 minutes or until they're golden and melty. Serve with gluten-free marinara sauce for dipping.

Gluten-Free Air-Fried Garlic Parmesan Chicken Wings

Ingredients:

- Chicken wings

- Gluten-free garlic powder, grated Parmesan cheese, and fresh parsley

- Olive oil

Instructions:

1. Toss the chicken wings in olive oil, garlic powder, and grated Parmesan cheese.

2. Preheat the air fryer and lightly grease the basket.

3. Arrange the chicken wings in a single layer and air fry at 375°F (190°C) for 25-30 minutes or until they're crispy and cooked through. Sprinkle with fresh parsley before serving.

Gluten-Free Air-Fried Avocado Fries

Ingredients:

- Avocado slices

- Gluten-free rice flour

- Eggs (or a dairy-free alternative)

- Gluten-free breadcrumbs

- Gluten-free ranch dressing (check for gluten-free)

Instructions:

1. Dredge the avocado slices in rice flour, dip in beaten eggs, and coat with gluten-free breadcrumbs.

2. Preheat the air fryer and lightly grease the basket.

3. Arrange the coated avocado slices in a single layer and air fry at 375°F (190°C) for 5-7 minutes or until they're crispy and golden. Serve with gluten-free ranch dressing for dipping.

Gluten-Free Air-Fried Stuffed Acorn Squash with Quinoa and Cranberries

Ingredients:

- Acorn squash, halved and seeds removed

- Cooked gluten-free quinoa

- Dried cranberries and chopped pecans

- Maple syrup (check for gluten-free)

Instructions:

1. In a bowl, combine cooked quinoa, dried cranberries, chopped pecans, and a drizzle of maple syrup.

2. Fill the acorn squash halves with the quinoa mixture.

3. Preheat the air fryer and air fry the stuffed acorn squash at 375°F (190°C) for 20-25 minutes, or until the squash is tender and the filling is heated through.

Gluten-Free Air-Fried Greek Chicken Souvlaki Skewers

Ingredients:

- Chicken breast or thigh, cubed

- Gluten-free Greek marinade (check for gluten-free)

- Cherry tomatoes, bell peppers, and red onion chunks

- Gluten-free tzatziki sauce (check for gluten-free)

Instructions:

1. Marinate the chicken pieces in gluten-free Greek marinade for about 30 minutes.

2. Thread the marinated chicken, cherry tomatoes, bell peppers, and red onion onto skewers.

3. Preheat the air fryer and air fry the skewers at 375°F (190°C) for 12-15 minutes, turning occasionally, until the chicken is cooked through.

4. Serve with gluten-free tzatziki sauce for dipping.

CHAPTER THREE

CONCLUSION

In conclusion, gluten-free air frying is not just a culinary technique; it's a delightful way to create flavorful and satisfying dishes for individuals with dietary sensitivities. By following the tips and tricks discussed, you can confidently embark on your gluten-free air frying journey.

Whether you're experimenting with alternative flours, embracing certified gluten-free ingredients, or mastering the art of adjusting cooking times, success in gluten-free air frying is attainable through practice and perseverance. The right combination of fresh, whole ingredients, balanced flavors, and the utilization of your air fryer's capabilities can lead to wonderfully crispy and gluten-free creations.

Remember, the key to success lies in maintaining awareness of cross-contamination risks, embracing creativity in your recipes, and continuously honing your skills in the gluten-free kitchen. As you explore the diverse world of gluten-free air frying, you'll discover an array of delicious and safe culinary experiences that delight both your palate and your well-being.

With a dash of innovation, a sprinkle of patience, and a dollop of understanding, you can embark on a gluten-free air frying journey that opens up a world of gluten-free possibilities and palate-pleasing delights. Happy cooking, and may your gluten-free air-fried meals always bring joy to your table.

Printed in Great Britain
by Amazon